OUT OF STEP

The Family, American Society, and the Christian Gospel

Wayne G. Boulton
Hope College

Foreword by John M. Mulder

UNIVERSITY
PRESS OF
AMERICA

Lanham • New York • London

BV
4526.2
.B674
1992

Copyright © 1992 by
University Press of America®, Inc.
4720 Boston Way
Lanham, Maryland 20706

3 Henrietta Street
London WC2E 8LU England

All rights reserved
Printed in the United States of America
British Cataloging in Publication Information Available

Biblical quotations, unless otherwise noted, are from the Revised
Standard Version of the Bible, copyright 1946, 1952, © 1971, 1973
by the Division of Christian Education of the National Council of
Churches of Christ in the U.S.A. and are used by permission.

Library of Congress Cataloging-in-Publication Data

Boulton, Wayne G.
Out of Step : The Family, American Society, and the
Christian Gospel / Wayne G. Boulton ; foreword by
John M. Mulder.
p.   cm.
Includes bibliographical references.
1. Family—United States—Religious life.
2. Family—United States.   I. Title.
BV4526.2.B674   1992
261.8′ 3585—dc20   91-37532 CIP

ISBN 0-8191-8501-9 (cloth : alk. paper)
ISBN 0-8191-8502-7 (pbk. : alk. paper)

The paper used in this publication meets the minimum requirements of
American National Standard for Information Sciences—Permanence
of Paper for Printed Library Materials, ANSI Z39.48–1984.

To

Mom and Dad:

Mary Granberry Boulton

and

Wayne Kelly Boulton (1911-1989)

"I was spying on the Kriegmans, envying them their happiness."

"That's the way we look to them, too. Don't worry about it. All families look great through windows."

J. UPDIKE
Roger's Version (1986)

ACKNOWLEDGEMENTS

Since childhood, I have believed that the family is always and everywhere a religious institution, a sacred unit. The essay before you is an attempt to make some Christian sense of that intuition.

As my friends and colleagues at Hope College can attest, composing this short book has been a long and a difficult road. These folks bear no responsibility for what I have written here; more than one of them, I believe, would contest some or even most of my conclusions. But I could not have done it without them. In my own Religion Department, I am surrounded by the best type of colleague----generous and critical----and I thank Barry Bandstra, Elton Bruins, Jenny Everts, Bob Palma, Al Verhey, Dennis Voskuil, and Boyd Wilson for their unfailing interest and support.

In higher education, help with a project is sometimes expressed informally---- a word of encouragement, the right question at the right time, a word of caution. Other Hope colleagues I would cite in this connection are Bill Cohen, Jane Dickie, Sander DeHaan, Bob Elder, Art Jentz, Don Luidens, Dave Myers, Jim Piers, Jack Ridl, Carol Simon, and John Shaughnessy. I teach about 250 students every year at Hope College; their contributions are hidden but enormous. I owe Karen Michmerhuizen a special note of thanks for her splendid secretarial assistance. My student assistant, Rameen Zahed, helped with the proofreading. And finally, Provost Nyenhuis and the College itself supported my work with two Summer Faculty Development Grants, and by funding a trip to Oxford University to study a phenomenon central to the argument of this book----secularization. When all is said and done, a liberal arts college is truly a remarkable organism.

But to display the community that got this book off the ground, I must cast a wider net. As he has done for so many less established ethicists, Duke's Stanley Hauerwas offered me his unique brand of encouragement. I can't count the number of probing discussions on the family I've had with Don Taylor, a Presbyterian layman from Grand Rapids and a great friend. Ray Anderson and Dennis Guernsey of Fuller Seminary have been conversation partners along the way. My former colleague Tom Kennedy, now of Valparaiso University, embodies Proverbs 27:17 ("Iron sharpens iron. . . .) for me, and has been a

vii

tremendous help. Librarian Paul Smith and the late Elton Eenigenberg of Western Seminary were gracious hosts to me during my short study leave at their institution, as was Principal McKane of St. Mary's College at the University of St. Andrews.

One of the elusive problems in family studies is getting the politics of family life right. More often than not, this is what Christians are in fact arguing about when they argue about the family. If Out of Step contributes anything helpful or important to the debate, I would observe that the original source probably goes back to a series of encounters I had in graduate school twenty years ago with a political science professor, John Hallowell of Duke University. Dr. Hallowell taught his students to respect the range and integrity of the political dimension of our common life, and even more to avoid confusing it with (while not separating it from) certain other dimensions----particularly the social, the moral, the psychological and the religious. I stand in his debt.

My own family, of course, has been the most formative and influential graduate school of all. Since I am an only child, this means my parents, to whom the book is dedicated, my wife, Vicki, our sons Matthew and Christopher, my grandparents, and the Rubin and Richardson families. If these loved ones have taught me anything worth passing on to family researchers of every type, it is this: don't rush to judgment. It is probably no accident that Out of Step goes to press as our youngest son finishes his senior year in high school and is leaving the nest. No matter how much you study the family, its mystery has a way of continuously opening up in front of you. So this book does not close the book on the family. Rather it is a series of "furrows in being," learned primarily from those close at hand, that aim at making the ineradicable mystery of family life----its sacredness----a little clearer.

Holland, Michigan
Summer 1991

PREFACE

In my neck of the woods, the crisis in American families today boils down to this. From the late 1920's until quite recently, mainstream Protestant churches in the United States have been addressing family issues with sense and savvy. Their assumptions----by and large----have been correct ones. They never adopted a sex-negative posture, but rather affirmed sexuality as a good gift of the Creator, as God's way of drawing us out of isolation and into companionship and communion. They have shown considerable interest in new empirical knowledge about the family and sexuality. Lacking any history that exalted virginity and celibacy over married life, mainstream Protestants rightly have interpreted marriage and family as high religious callings. On the other hand, since marriage is not viewed as a sacrament, these same Protestants tended to view divorce as a grave act but usually a permissible one. And they held that the fundamental aims of Christian marriage must include the expression of faithful love, and not just procreation and the prevention of sin.

Then beginning in the late 1960's, a period of explosive change rocked these churches to their roots. They began shrinking; between 1965 and 1990, my own Presbyterian Church lost over 30% of its membership! Their seminaries started to become the more diverse places they are today, encouraging dialogue with Roman Catholic biblical scholarship, with black and feminist critiques of the church, with process and liberation theologies----leading to a certain blurring of theological identity. The struggle between various groups for dominance inside the camp became more and more visible. Family issues began to take a back seat; the social pronouncements of these denominations turned increasingly toward systemic injustice and appeals for political change.

A number of these trends reached a zenith of sorts in the spring of 1991, when a wide-ranging Presbyterian report on sexuality----three years in the making----caused an instant furor, created unprecedented interest in the national media, and seemed to help almost no one.[1] We had a "crisis in the family" all right. More precisely, it was in the interpretation of family life that we had a crisis. Families all across the country began to wonder what had happened to that Protestant tradition that once had been so helpful.

This book is one person's attempt to pick up that tradition and display it again. To no one's surprise, it may be difficult to recognize. Much has transpired in the last thirty years. As we can see in William Johnson Everett's superb Blessed Be The Bond (Fortress, 1985), Christian studies of the family today should be characterized by the following three features.

The first is a critical appropriation of the social sciences. In any book about family "sacredness," it is of great importance to review carefully what social scientists mean when they speak of religion and social structure. If the family turns out to be a sacred unit, this is a significant insight into all families, and not just into peculiar realities of particular churches. We Christians must learn to speak more carefully about religion. To call families sacred or religious is not necessarily to call them Christian. And with the help of social science, we need to resist the tendency to take our eyes off larger social forces as we tinker with concrete family problems----accommodating ourselves too thoroughly to that wrenching series of dislocations in family life brought about by the industrial transformation of society.

A second feature of Christian family studies is that they need to be ecumenical. There is no longer any excuse for a Protestant to remain ignorant of the contribution of the Roman Catholic tradition on the family, for liberal Christians to dismiss the evangelical contribution, and so on. As a Protestant, I have been stunned by the richness of the Catholic sense of my subject, and believe that Christians of every stripe henceforth need to approach the family together rather than separately.

The final feature of adequate Christian family studies today is that they should be ecumenical in an even wider, broader sense----particularly with respect to Judaism and the Hebrew Scriptures. As is well known, the Jewish appreciation of the family is extraordinary. What Christians call the "Old Testament" has become the single most influential pro-family document ever written. The feminist school of interpretation notwithstanding, the Christian community needs to struggle to let the Old Testament speak with its own integrity and power on the family, and not rush to Christianize or modernize it. For it is this distinct tradition that gives some balance to what New Testament writers have to say about the family, and provides perhaps the only context in which Jesus' warnings about family idolatry make complete sense.

Like a much-used, trustworthy compass, the words of Jesus point to the great challenge facing families today. The challenge is indeed the archaic one of idolatry all dressed up in twentieth century clothing. But the term "idolatry" here points to a larger reality than simply the investment of the family itself with too much significance.[2] The more subtle nemesis of contemporary families is a new and virulent form of what the ancient Church Fathers called "paganism." We are more likely to encounter it as a social cancer within the family than as an idolatry of the family. Its essence is the attempt to define life and meaning apart from God.

Such are the contours of this book. May the tradition from which it springs, though weakened momentarily, gain strength in the years to come.

NOTES

[1]While Keeping Body and Soul Together: Sexuality, Spirituality, and Social Justice (Louisville, KY: Stated Clerk of the General Assembly, 1991) is a document with considerable strengths accompanying its limitations, sensitivity to historic Christian insights into family life is not among them. See Epilogue.

[2]Cf. Janet Fishburn, Confronting the Idolatry of Family (Nashville, TN: Abingdon, 1991).

CONTENTS

Acknowledgments   vii

Preface   ix

Foreword   xv

Introduction   xvii

Chapter 1 WHAT IS HAPPENING TO THE FAMILY?   1

    Placing the Family
    Defining the Family
    Is the Modern Family in Trouble?
    Family Piety and Christian Faith

Chapter 2 THE CULTS SEND A WARNING   15

    The Holy Family of Rev. Moon
    The Eternal Family of the Mormons
    The Hidden Challenge of the Cults

Chapter 3 A FAMILY THAT HURTS CHILDREN   23

    Down with Hierarchy
    Ostrich Nurture
    The Biblical Corrective

Chapter 4 A FAMILY THAT HURTS WIVES   35

        The Prison of Domesticity
        The Feminist Critique
        The Biblical Critique
        Marriage Transformed by Christ

Chapter 5 A FAMILY THAT HURTS HUSBANDS AND   47
           GRANDPARENTS

        Families in Union Park
        The Chief Victims
        The Strategies

Chapter 6 A FAMILY THAT HURTS THE WORLD   59

        Helping Our Children
        Helping Our Marriages
        Helping the Earth

Chapter 7 FAMILY, KINGDOM AND CHURCH   69

        The Mystery of the Kingdom
        The Mystery of the Church
        The Mystery of Faith

Epilogue   79

About the Author   83

FOREWORD

Out of Step is an important and noteworthy book. Written by a Presbyterian minister who is a social ethicist, it is a call to Presbyterians and mainstream Protestants to put the family back on the ethical agenda of the church.

Some might find it strange that the family dropped from view in mainstream Protestantism. In one sense, it probably never did. The reality of congregational life makes one keenly aware of families. Births, baptism, weddings, and funerals are all profoundly familial occasions. But there are other experiences that involve families as well--divorces, spouse abuse, child abuse, parental abuse. The family has virtually unlimited potential for being an avenue of God's grace and an environment of racial evil and suffering.

But mainstream Protestant denominations have largely ignored the escalating problems in American family life since the 1960's. As Don S. and Carol Browning have declared, "For the past 30 years, these churches have been timid and inarticulate about the growing family crisis. They have let the family issue fall into the hands of reactionary political and religious forces to the right or radical cultural forces to the left" (Christian Century, August 7-14, 1991, p. 747).

Wayne Boulton's book will help restore the issue of the family to theological and ethical discussion. The book draws on a variety of scholarship--biblical studies, Jewish, Roman Catholic, and Protestant reflections, feminist and evangelical thought, and social scientific and historical research.

Readers will find much here to ponder. They may also discover new controversies. But they will not be bored. Wayne Boulton writes out of a deep Christian commitment and passionate concern to renew and make whole the

xv

fragmented family of modern America. He can help us begin again the conversation about the family and its capacity to transmit human love and divine grace.

JOHN M. MULDER

President and Professor of Historical Theology
Louisville Presbyterian Theological Seminary

INTRODUCTION

*"The dreariness of the family's spiritual
landscape passes belief."*

A. BLOOM[1]

Is the American family in decline? The answer appears to be "No."

A recent Gallup Poll indicates that mobility, divorce, and changing lifestyles are not preventing Americans from honoring their family ties.[2] On the contrary, the overwhelming majority of the 1,250 adults interviewed had stayed in touch with their extended families over the course of their lifetimes.

Furthermore, our families are not even terribly scattered geographically. A full two-thirds of adults with living parents live within an hour's drive of Mom or Dad, while 13 percent have a parent living with them in the same household. With very few exceptions, Americans today seem to enjoy being with family members and wish they had more time to spend with them.

To be sure, our households are smaller than they used to be. With people getting married later in life, divorce rates remaining high and an elderly population becoming more affluent, there are not as many people in the average home today. More people are deciding to live alone, and fewer are living under the same roof with their cousins, aunts and uncles.

Modern communication networks and more affordable transportation help bridge the distance between family members. The poll showed that even when separated by great distances, parents and children (86 percent), brothers and sisters (13 percent), and grandparents and grandchildren (46 percent) keep in touch at least monthly by telephone. Half of those interviewed talk with their parents once a week or more, and 70 percent were able to attend at least one large family social gathering in the previous year.

One mildly disturbing finding of the poll probably will not surprise us: The burden of maintaining strong extended families in America today continues to fall on women. Put differently, the poll attests to the strength of the mother-daughter bond and appears to confirm the special nature of the mother-child relationship.

Young women are much more likely than their male counterparts to rely most on a parent for advice in a crisis----and that parent is almost always the mother. Among adults under thirty years of age, 31 percent of both genders confide in their mothers vs. only 6 percent in their fathers. Sons and daughters both report more difficulties in getting along with their fathers than with their mothers.

Though young husbands and wives feel equally connected to their extended families, the proportion of men who rate their family of origin highly important drops after age thirty, and does not rebound among older men. Among women, the rating remains constant. This is reflected in the fact that both husbands and wives report spending more time with the wife's family than with the husband's. Perhaps the old adage is true----"A daughter is a daughter all of her life, a son is a son until he takes a wife."

Despite this imbalance, it would be easy to conclude from the poll that the American family today is strong. But such a conclusion would be misleading. The dis-ease that many of us feel about family life in the late twentieth century is not an illusion generated by right wing fantasies. Though the American family is far from dead, it is clearly in danger----a danger peculiar to our time. The poll is correct in what it reports. The problem is that it does not report enough.

First, it leaves out historical perspective. The American family today is structurally much weaker than it was in 1800. At that time, family units were the center of economic production in our largely rural economy. This is no longer the case.

The poll also remains silent about the current divorce rate and its impact on marriage. We now live in a nation in which marital discord is almost as common as marital stability, and in which----particularly in certain age groups----divorce and separation are encountered so frequently as to be unexceptional. If you are between the ages of 35 and 54 in America today, you are part of a generation that ushered in the largest increase in the rate of divorce ever recorded. (This was between 1965 and 1975, when the rate nearly doubled.)

Introduction

The poll doesn't look at the individualism and competitiveness that pervade the industrial, urbanized setting of today's families. The values of modern democracy and commercialism are not always friendly to the family. While our marketplace and voting booth call for a recognition of individual achievement and rights, the family insists that individual interests be subordinate to the group. While our democratic society wants to judge each person on the basis of merit, the family denies merit as the basis of inclusion or support.

And finally, the American family is in some trouble today because of the widespread failure to recognize what it is. The book before you is a direct response to this failure. As Elton Trueblood said 50 years ago about marriage, seeing into the heart of an institution is the best way to begin resolving our practical difficulties with it. Trueblood was right that a sacred calling is at the heart of marriage. Likewise, the family is actually a religious institution---- always has been, always will be.

Every religion in the world recognizes this, and consequently all religions pay a great deal of attention to family life. The same survey discovered that when religion plays an important part in the life of a husband or wife, that person is much less likely to have experienced severe marital discord. This finding holds no matter how young or old the couple, and no matter which religion they endorse.

This is so, I believe, simply because the essential purposes of family are all religious ones----to stem pride and self-centeredness, to teach us that we are loved and that we are lovers, to open our souls to a higher power. It was not for nothing that the Puritans called the family the "littlest church." In a word, the family is sacred.

The loss of the sacred in the modern world has had quite an impact on family life, as those familiar with the Roman Catholic Christian tradition can attest. As a Presbyterian, it took me some time to realize that Catholic prohibitions of abortion and of artificial methods of birth control are neither as legalistic nor as faintly archaic as they may sound to Protestant ears. In fact, they constitute a profound protest against a growing unwillingness among modern (particularly Western) couples to welcome children into their midst. Personally, I don't agree with either prohibition strictly interpreted; but these vintage Roman Catholic laws mean much more than they say. They warn against an increase of selfishness amidst unparalled affluence. They warn about a growing----let's be candid---- distaste for children, such drains on our chosen lifestyles and careers. These prohibitions help to expose perhaps the most dangerous <u>moral</u> tendency in today's families.

But we need to look deeper. The sadness and hurt that so many family members feel is the <u>anguish of religious loss</u>, the pain of the disinherited. The modern family is in exile, out of step with a desacralized, technological society.[3] A family is a little society that longs for heaven; God sets things up that way. Any family that has lost its anchor in transcendent values is adrift----often without knowing it. A family without faith has lost track of what it is.

As world communism enters a period of decline, the need to recover family sacredness may never have been more imperative. The 1989 collapse of communist governments was so swift as to be breathtaking, and can be explained in more than one way. Some read it politically, claiming that it signals the final triumph of democracy over its great modern rival, Marxism. Others see the decline of communism as a religious victory of the human spirit in a spiritual struggle against repressive public policy.

While partly true, both explanations are a tad too hopeful, almost naive, and neither of them gives a sufficient account of what a world without communism has <u>lost</u>.[4] Many assume that when the East appears to want what the West has, this is a uniformly happy prospect. But it ain't necessarily so. <u>Playboy</u> magazine, for example, is now set up for publishing in Hungary----a move advertised in <u>The New York Times</u> with the words "Exporting the American Dream." What will replace the ideological materialism of the communists? What if it is simply the hedonistic, practical materialism of the West?

It is easy to forget that what is now evaporating from the European landscape is a kind of faith----a belief in something larger than the individual, a conviction that one should devote oneself to this something, even die for it. To be sure, Marxist-Leninist communism attacked religion, but at the same time it is a product of a world that felt the need for a transcendent vision. Before its moral capital gave out, Marxist-Leninism traded on a sense of moral outrage at the injustices of the world, and called for a revolution to create a better one. In an age fast losing its capacity to live for anything above the level of private life, communism has represented a kind of survival of the longing for transcendent truth and justice.

Now the massive communist experiment as a whole appears to be succumbing. Perhaps we should not mourn its passing. But let us not be naive about the societies that will succeed it. The eclipse of communist ideology is taking place in a world of increasingly non-transcendent, desacralized values. And this is where the family finds itself today.

The family remains a place where sinners live, as it has always been, but family sin in the contemporary world is shaped by the conditions of a sacred unit-in-exile. Sometimes the family becomes a "sacred cow" and consumes too much (Chapter 6). Other times it becomes confused about its own sacred structure, and parents lose their courage (Chapter 3). And yet other times, it closes too securely around Mom, Dad, and the kids, and cuts off Grandpa and Grandma (Chapter 5).

If the analysis here is even partly correct, few institutions are more important for families in our time than the Christian church (Chapter 7).[5] It has a long history of examining and evaluating sacred realities. A species of family itself, the church is nicely positioned to address the root cause of family discontent----sin. But most of all, it is the institution best suited to call families beyond themselves toward that for which every family is a community of preparation----the kingdom or "family" of God.

NOTES

[1]Allan Bloom, The Closing of the American Mind (New York: Simon and Schuster, 1987), p. 57.

[2]Leslie C. McAreny, ed., The Gallup Report, Nos. 284, 285 (May, June 1989). The survey was conducted May 15-18, 1989.

[3]This book is written from the standpoint that there is truth in the controversial "secularization thesis." The version I support is presented in Chs. 6 and 7. In my view, it is no accident that an influential, recent work with real insight into family life is written by authors thoroughly familiar with secularization theory: Habits of the Heart: Individualism and Commitment in American Life by Robert Bellah et al (Berkeley, CA: University of California Press, 1985), esp. Chapter 4.

[4]See A. J. Conyers, "Communism's Collapse: The Receding Shadow of Transcendence," <u>Christian Century</u> (May 2, 1990), pp. 466-467.

[5]I am not suggesting that other religions have nothing to offer the family today. Indeed, the Christian church----with its profound dependence upon Judaism in this connection in its Holy Scriptures----is <u>certainly</u> not in a position to make such an assertion. I lack the training required to evaluate the contributions of non-Christian religions in this regard.

Chapter 1

WHAT IS HAPPENING TO THE FAMILY?

"The Greeks are . . . attached to their own,
but they know the difference between the love
of their own and the truth. "

L. KASS[1]

Once upon a time, a Persian King (Darius) called together a group of Greeks and Indians, and proceeded to have a little fun at their expense. He was well aware that among the world's peoples, sacred conventions and customs are not only powerful, but powerfully different. In his time, the Greeks burned the bodies of their dead, whereas this particular group of Indians ate the bodies of their fathers when they died. Darius offered to pay the Greeks anything they wanted if they would simply change their funeral practices and eat their own dead. The Greeks refused, saying that no sum of money could tempt them to do such a thing. He then made a similar offer to the Indians, asking them to burn the bodies of their fathers at death. According to Herodotus, the Indians "exclaimed aloud, and bade him forbear such language."[2]

Such is the situation facing any theorist of the family. Like funerals, the family and familial routines are universal; all societies have them. And again like funerals, the customs and conventions governing family life are both powerful and powerfully different. In this last decade of the twentieth century, with the debate about "family values" swirling around us, the point almost makes itself. Under the leadership of psychologist James Dobson, Christian traditionalists are attacking permissiveness in families and gaining a renewed sense of the meaning of loving leadership and discipline in Christian homes (see Chapter 3). But on the other side, under the equally effective leadership of the likes of Virginia Mollenkott and James Nelson, more liberal Christians identify the hierarchial traditional family as the problem rather than the solution, for it encourages the oppression of wives by husbands and children by parents (see Chapter 4).

Funeral and family practices are alike in one more way.   In every society, both are normally loaded with piety and religion.   Here we have a fact about the family which, while evident, is certainly not simple.   The book before you is an attempt to make some Christian sense of it.   My argument is that the sacredness of the family is at once its central feature and the primary source of confusion about it.   For the family is sacred in more than one sense.   It is a sacred relic, a holdover from a distant, less individualistic age; it has a sacred center or structure, the hierarchical relation of nurture between parents and children; and it also can be a "sacred cow," betraying a tendency----exposed by Jesus----to make itself into an idol.

So at the outset, the position of a family theorist is not too different from that of a rebellious teenager.   We begin with the suspicion that even our own family doesn't always tell the truth about itself, but rather invests its particular customs with an almost "religious" ultimacy so as to place them beyond criticism.[3]   As college students tell me again and again, they always assumed their own family was "normal," no matter how crippled or dysfunctional its actual state.

Put philosophically, the family often confuses its nature with its conventions. Remember the Greeks and the Indians.   Constructing a theory of the family, therefore, is never an easy task.   Its main requirement is the aim of this chapter: to push beyond family conventions, no matter how powerful, and uncover something of the family's nature.

Placing the Family

Perhaps all of us are a bit intimidated by our own families.   Extending backward and forward in time, with members scattered hither and yon but bound fast by ties that span continents, the family is probably the most ancient, the most powerful and certainly the most durable institution known to humankind.   We often experience the power of family as "fate" because our free will has here such a limited role----none at all in the selection of our natural parents, and precious little in the choice of in-laws.   Even those of us who get along with our in-laws find the family to be an imperious presence, not only shaping us in our childhood (nurture), but providing much of the "quarry" from which we are shaped (nature). Because of its depth and range, the boundaries of family spread beyond any single academic field of inquiry, such as psychology or political science.

In every civilization, the institution of family life intersects with religion.[4] The family unit as a whole is frequently deified, as in the Homeric extended patriarchal family of Zeus and Hera with their variously begotten offspring, or in the ancient Egyptian trio of Osiris, Isis and Horus.   Though Westerners often forget it, the oldest and most widely spread religious practice of all is probably the veneration of ancestors, a rite that depends squarely on projection grounded in the experience of family.

Historically, organized religion has provided massive support and affirmation for family life, defending the family against a wide range of cultured and ascetic detractors. In America today, the pro-family posture of religion is most evident in the Jewish and Roman Catholic traditions, though I would be hard pressed to name any orthodox religious group unconcerned with strengthening the family. There is a good and sufficient reason for this. All major religions have long recognized that for good or for ill, the family is a formidable and virtually irreplaceable shaper of souls----the souls of parents as well as the souls of children. In a sense, religions and families are in the same business; and the respect for family life among religious leaders is often mixed with not a little awe.

Christianity above all has stressed that families shape souls for good and for ill. It is of the essence of family that it is a provisional unit, a training ground for the kingdom or family of God. What families need most is a different sort of provisional unit that understands the family's purpose, and is independent enough to stand over against families, admonishing them when they fail. Widespread anxieties about the family in our revolutionary age only aggravate the problem of making families intelligible to themselves. The best candidate for this role of instructing families, I believe, is organized religion. For without consistent religious instruction, the crucial distinction between one's own family (tribe, nation) and the family of God becomes blurred, and families lose their moorings. Thus in complex and curious ways, the fate of the family today is bound up intimately with the fate of religion, and in particular with the strength of the church.[5]

Defining the Family

The family comes in a variety of social forms, which can be bewildering. The most common form in the West has been the nuclear family, where mother and father live with their children----and apart from other relatives----under the same roof. There are a growing number of single parent families. There are blended families, into which both husband and wife bring children from previous marriages. When composed of two or more nuclear family units living in the same household, the family in question is termed a "joint family." If these units live in the same local area, we have a form with yet another name---the extended family. Receiving increased attention are gay and lesbian couples who commonly form families by raising children supplied by a previous marriage or through adoption.

The family is a sacred unit. No matter what its social form or historical context, the family is an arena in which the absolute (the unconditioned; God) is normally----though not universally----encountered. The family is sacred space; the so-called "sacredness of the hearth" is a reality. Like all sacred spaces, however, you can traverse it without sensing it or knowing where you are.[6]

The heart of the familial unit is the relationship between parents and children. Though it is frequently confused with the institution of marriage, the family is a sacred unit to be understood primarily as the seat of origination rather than as a type of affiliation. This is an alternative to the most common Western definition of family as a conjugal, affiliative unit of parents and children with the marriage of the parents at its foundation.

Put differently, the structure of family life has two base lines or axes----the spousal axis and the parental axis----with the second being the more basic of the two. The spousal line is constituted by the choice of mate, sexual attraction, sexual intercourse and the whole range of spousal intimacy. The parental axis is the impulse to protect and prefer one's own progeny. The sacredness of family is usually experienced along these two lines, either extending out to cousins, aunts, nieces, etc., or more typically moving along the parental axis to grandparents, grandchildren, etc.

In a word, the modern family is defined here as a weakened consanguineal unit based on blood or adoptive relationships, rather than as a conjugal one. To be sure, the conjugal element has become stronger in modern industrial democracies, but this has not changed the family qua family. Though normally associated with marriage, it is always distinct from marriage.

All around the world, not only is the family usually regarded as prior to the state (set apart or "sacred" from a political point of view), but it is also the site of a cluster of profoundly sensed obligations, attachments and loyalties. We call these deferences to family "piety," using the same word that we use to describe our deferences to God. Indeed, there is a connection between them. In the helpful language of James Gustafson, the biosocial needs out of which the family emerges constitute one of the basic "patterns and processes of interdependence of life in this world"----a sign of "the ultimately divine empowering and ordering of life, . . . of the radical dependence of human life on powers that are prior, ultimately of dependence on God."[7]

To see the political and social dimension of family sacredness, it is wise to look East, where the kinship system generally is stronger and less qualified by a Western individualism partly sponsored by Christianity. Confucianism provides us with a perfect example. For Confucius (551-479 B.C.), the deference of children to their parents (particularly sons to fathers) is considered fundamental for life as a whole----for all other family relationships (such as husband and wife), for economic relationships, for civic relationships, for relations with the natural world and with the gods. According to the Confucian Classic of Filial Piety, "serving parents when alive with love and affection, and when dead with grief and sorrow----this completely exhausts the basic duties of living men."[8]

Note well: to call families sacred or even religious or pious is not to call them Christian. The religiosity of family life is often subtle, and can include all four phases of the evolution of religion over time.[9] In its primal stage, religion is tribal or oriented to a single ethnic group. Its spirituality is deeply integrated with all phases of life; this type of belief system usually emerges among non-literate peoples. Archaic religion is the religion of larger scale, stratified and more complex societies . . . with their "earth mothers" and "royal fathers." Few such religions remain in existence today, though Japanese Shinto would be one example. In the next phase, classical religions such as Judaism, Christianity, and Islam appear on the world's stage. They mark the first appearance of a religious rejection of "the world" and an extremely negative, dualistic evaluation of society. In the final or modern phase, religion is significantly altered through its interaction with industry and science, becoming more positively inclined toward the created order. It is increasingly individualistic and egalitarian, and tends toward skepticism regarding miracles and magic.

My hunch is that many modern families are repositories of archaic and particularly primal religion. The difficulty we have in sensing the religious qualities of these families is the same difficulty moderns have in seeing any religion at all in the pervasive, relatively simple and often ancestor-venerating spirituality of tribal peoples. Noting his tribe's lack of religious institutions, the Apache leader Geronimo protested: "We have no churches, no sabbaths, no holidays, yet we worshipped. Sometimes the whole tribe would assemble to sing and pray, sometimes less----perhaps only two or three."[10]

If we restrict religion exclusively to its Christian form, we are not going to see other potent sorts of family religiosity. It is not for nothing that sexual intercourse is often called "the pagan sacrament." Before classical religions imposed their theologies (with mixed success) on family life, the most common religion was the veneration of ancestors, and the most sacred of duties was procreation. Furthermore, only through the rediscovery of family religion will we regain clarity about the ancient hostility between Christianity and the family, a conflict in which Christianity has been largely victorious in the West. The conflict is clear in the New Testament, which displaces the family with the ecclesia (church) as the communal center of religious interest in this life. In sharp contrast to the Hebrew Scriptures, the New Testament gives more attention to marriage than to family, for the marital bonds of promise are seen as a closer parallel to the new bond with Christ (Ephesians 5:31-32) than are familial bonds of blood.

Is the Modern Family in Trouble?

In periods of rapid social change, such as our own, it is easy to forget the Christian view of the family as a social structure marked by sin, i.e., that it has always been "in trouble." A few years ago, John Scanzoni warned against the common tendency of every age, rooted in family piety, to idealize the generation immediately preceding it.[11] Conservatives, in particular, think naturally of "the good old days"----forgetting the bad things while magnifying the good. Such an approach is not exactly a dependable guide in assessing the state of American families. Yet we adopt it all the time.

For example, the rising divorce rate is often cited as proof that the family is in decline. There were relatively few divorces before the Civil War in America, and the divorce rate has been rising ever since. So in the good old nineteenth century, marriages at least seem to have been more stable than they are today. But were they? Historians now recognize the fact that while legal divorces were relatively rare a century ago, desertion ("the poor man's divorce") was probably practiced much more widely. During the expansion of the Western frontier, giving one's family "the slip" and never returning home could be done with consummate ease. With no FBI and no social security numbers, tracing a marital deserter was virtually impossible. Nineteenth century families may not have been as stable as we like to think.

Another example is the curious idea that because of the pace of modern life, we care much less about our children today than our ancestors did. Modern mothers, it is alleged, have become materialistic and selfish. They go to work and leave their children in nursery school or with sitters. At night, kids are put in front of TV so the adults can talk. Parents, we suspect, just don't have the time for children they once had. But what time did they once have? Before the Industrial Revolution, most women were married to farmers or shopkeepers, and worked right alongside their husbands all day. Struggling to survive, ordinary families lacked the option of assigning one of their members to full-time motherhood. If American children today rarely have full-time mothers, and some suffer for it, the good old days did not provide them either.

Taking Ecclesiastes 7:10 as his text ("Say not, Why were the former days better than these?' For it is not from wisdom that you ask this."), Scanzoni sees things differently. There may be as much (or more) promise as peril in the many changes experienced by American families today.[12] Change is not necessarily crisis. Not only is the contrast between today's and yesterday's families less marked than some would have it, but precisely those trends tending to weaken the family (e.g. the divorce rate, less stringent divorce laws, a new awareness of family violence, etc.) reflect the strengthening of another favorite American institution: the individual.

From the vantage point of individual husbands and wives, Scanzoni argues, the past turns out to be less wonderful than we thought. Before the late nineteenth century when divorce became relatively common in America, the family took priority over the individuals within it. There was no such thing as a divorce on the grounds of "mutual incompatibility." Yes, the divorce rate was low, but at what cost in terms of individual satisfaction and fulfillment? Similarly, the topic of intrafamily violence was hardly mentioned a century ago. The silence about spouse and child abuse has been broken today, but the reason is surely not that family violence was invented in the 20th century! Rather, women are gradually rejecting the idea that family is always and everywhere more important than their individual rights and well-being. And this, surely, is progress.

There is no doubt, however, that much of the change families have been experiencing in the last century and a half involves loss. The primary loss has been in the dimension that sociologists dub "social function." Family units were once the center of economic production; they no longer are.[13] The clan long ago stopped providing armed defense and physical protection for its members; the police and the army do this now. The family used to be the primary educational agent for the young, but that was before the public school. Care for the family's poor, weak, and wounded is now provided largely by public agencies and by a distinctly modern institution----the social security system. One important meaning of modern individualism is that membership in a family is no longer necessary for political success. Having children used to be financially desireable, for they quickly became part of the family's labor force and provided security for aging parents. Now children rarely work for their parents and----as every modern parent knows----each child has come to represent a substantial financial burden.

So the family in America is a slimmer, scaled-down and more fragile institution than in the past. In a structural sense, it is definitely "weaker," i.e., more subject to dissolution. Yet what is not clear is that this loss of function has been crippling or even critical. For the family continues to provide what no other institution offers: emotional and physical intimacy, nurture and support for children, and affection between spouses. Once one assumes (as I do) that these functions were meant to be primary in family life, then it is quite possible that the modern family is the first one to shed its dead weight. It is free to perform its primary purposes without the internal distractions of property, production and other material considerations.

The modern American family, which emerged in the late eighteenth and early nineteenth century, displays a slim "lightness" reflecting precisely such an intention.[14] The marriage that initiated it was based upon love and mutual respect between the partners, not the choice(s) of their families of origin. The woman in the marriage enjoyed an increasing degree of influence within the family. Her primary role was the care of the children and the maintenance of the home, whereas her husband spent most of his time working at a different location. As mistress of the home, she was perceived by society as the moral superior of her husband, though his legal and social inferior. The focus and resources of both parents turned increasingly toward the rearing of children. Children were now perceived as sharply different from adults, deserving not only material support but love and solicitude as well.[15] And lastly, the size of this modern family is smaller than in previous centuries----a change with consequences for both fathers and mothers, but particularly for women.

In sum, what do we have here? We have a family struggling to turn more toward its own central purpose: to offer nurture and support to its members. Even if we are not completely happy with this modern form of the family, it is not altogether likely that we would embrace an alternative. Slimmer does not necessarily mean worse.

The threat facing families today derives from another source. The family has been fundamentally out of step with the values most closely identified with the last two centuries of Western history: equality, individualism and meritocracy. Since the American and French Revolutions and the rise of industrial capitalism, the family has found itself increasingly in a hostile world. Where modern democracies have emphasized equality, the family has consistently repudiated it. Even in the "companionate" family described above, hierarchy prevailed among father, mother and children. Down to the present day, few families treat their own members equally. Where modern society calls for a recognition of individualism, the family insists that individual interests be subordinate to the group. Where our society wants to judge each person on the basis of merit, the family denies merit as a basis of inclusion or support.

This tension between the family and modern society shows no sign of evaporating. The family will continue to be embattled. But the very peculiarity of the family in this connection is perhaps the deepest source of its continuing appeal. As an historian has noted:

The family . . . is an anti-individualistic institution. . . . For at least two centuries, the best known alternative to the individualism, competitiveness, and egoism that infuse the modern, industrial and urban world has been the family. That has been its strongest appeal as individualism spread from country to country in the wake of commercial and industrial capitalism. . . . That is also why all the great utopian visions of the 19th and 20th centuries from Marxism, which is the most familiar, to the hippies of yesterday, have taken the family as their model of human order. . . . In short, aside from the evidence that Americans still consider family a central institution in their lives, the very values for which it has stood over the years suggest that it will endure.[16]

Family Piety and the Christian Faith

In the New Testament, there is a curious "double attitude" toward religion that provides a decisive insight into families today. A positive approach to religion can be glimpsed in the writings of both Paul and John. Though his spirit is described as "provoked within him" at the many idols he encounters in the city of Athens (Acts 17:16), the Apostle Paul speaks to a small, cultivated audience on the Areopagus Hill and compliments them on their religion. Among other shrines in Athens, Paul says, he had found an altar dedicated "to an unknown God" (Acts 17:23). This God he will preach to them. Among the characteristics of this Creator are that He is not far from us and that we are His children, Paul states, quoting Greek religious writers to make his points (Acts 17:27-28). Likewise, a sentence in the Prologue to John's Gospel reads: "The true light that enlightens every man was coming into the world" (John 1:9, my emphasis).

The meaning of these passages is that there is a certain knowledge of God given to everyone, even in a "pagan" world. As Paul says elsewhere (Romans 1:19-20; 2:14-15), the possibility of knowing God is available through contemplating the works of creation and through attending to the inner moral law written in our hearts. Inside every person, the Divine Logos is working to give light and life, which points to the glimpses of truth and genuine knowledge of God scattered throughout all religions.

On the other hand, the New Testament equally insists that religion is always and everywhere subject to sin and marked by the grossest of errors and distortion. Because it is the religion of fallen human beings, it has become false religion----a virtual playground of demonic and evil powers. Thus the same Paul writes in his first letter to the Corinthians: "What pagans sacrifice, they sacrifice to demons and not to God. I do not want you to become partners with demons" (10:20). "Is there a fellowship between light and darkness? Is there a concord between

Christ and Belial? . . . Can there be an agreement between the temple of God and the idols? For we are the temple of God. . . ." (6:14-16).

This dual New Testament attitude toward religion is exactly what is called for in our approach to the religion of the family. For one cannot help but be struck by a fundamental duality running through all family religiosity. Some of it is pure, fragile, wonderfully human, beautiful, open to the world and to God. And some of it is morally perverse, devious, stubborn, proud, pathetic, violent, and closed in on itself.[17]

While never denying that the family is sacred, the New Testament gives to this social fact a new precision. When we sense familial sacredness, what we actually are responding to is the creation of God. The undeniably sacred qualities of mom, the hearth, etc. are derivative. The name of every family on earth and even in heaven, Paul writes, comes from God the Father (Ephesians 3:14-15). God is the Author of all parenthood.

But the most distinctive New Testament clarification of familial sacredness is that it is provisional. Along with singleness and celibacy, marriage and family point beyond themselves toward the kingdom of God. Each of these paths are revealed as essentially callings----vocations intended to contribute to the upbuilding of a particular kind of a community in the world. In a decisive break with Judaism, Paul suggests that singleness may have a certain superiority to marriage in this connection (I Corinthians 7:8, 26-27).

As a general rule, then, the job of Christians is to be simultaneously allies and critics of the family . . . and in particular, of familial religion. We will see that by and large, the resources needed for this task are already present in the Christian tradition. Christians have been carrying on a significant debate about family religiosity since the Reformation. In its sacralization of the earthly family of Jesus (through the elevation of Mary), its classification of marriage as a sacrament, its stand against divorce, its insistence that marriage be open to children and its principled opposition of abortion, the Roman Catholic tradition provides the basis to affirm what is positive in family religion from a Christian perspective. In its refusal to elevate Mary, its rejection of marriage as a sacrament, its subordination of procreation to unitive love in marriage and its hesitancy about opposing abortion on principle, the Protestant tradition provides a basis to criticize what needs exposing in family religion today.[18]

The book before you moves back and forth between these two poles. On the positive side, we argue that the sacredness of the family is under fire in the contemporary West, and in need of defense. Certain modern cults seem more aware of this than mainstream Christians (Chapter 2). Each family has a sacred structure (Chapter 3), and therefore should be protected as part of the natural environment we all need to be healthy (Chapter 6). More negatively, the impact of a certain type of modern family on women (Chapter 4) and on the elderly (Chapter 5) is badly in need of exposure and change.

Because of its very nature, the family presents us all with a dual challenge. On the one hand, there is a profound connection between the quality of our family ties and the moral truth about ourselves. If we are to ever learn to care for others, we must first learn to love those we are "stuck with" by accident of birth. Even family members we don't like are irrevocably ours. Only when we learn to care for our family, writes Stanley Hauerwas, "will love be understood not simply as attraction for those who are like us, but also as regard and respect for those we would not have chosen but to whom we find ourselves tied."[19]

And yet as Leon Kass suggests, the distinction between the love of our own and the truth is a crucial one. A rush to defend and heal our families pervades almost every sector of American society today, and threatens to push Christians further and further away from the New Testament. The great challenge facing Christian theologians of the family is to focus less on our anxiety-driven social programs, and more on following Jesus. Christ had no wife, no children. His famous "hard sayings" on the family do not go over too well in the current climate. The overall New Testament posture on families is not so much to comfort as to confront them, calling families to Christ and challenging them to participate in the larger family of God.

NOTES

[1]Leon R. Kass, Toward a More Natural Science (New York: The Free Press, 1985), p. 296. The passage from Herodotus, quoted in full on p. 281, suggests that Kass's preference for the Greeks may not be completely shared by the ancient historian.

[2]Herodotus, Histories, Book III. trans. by G. Rawlinson (New York: Random House, 1942), p. 230.

[3]Raised in the 1950's, I can think of no more pungent exposure of the idolatry of family at a particular historical moment than Philip Wylie's attack on "momism" in A Generation of Vipers (New York: Farrer and Rinehard, Inc., 1942).

[4]It could be argued that communist states constitute an exception here, though I do not believe they do. Remember that religion need not be organized to be real, and that even if we had more conclusive data before 1989, recent changes in the Soviet Union and China have been so far-reaching that any judgment should be tentative at this point. The most insightful analyst of the relation between family and religion is probably the Australian anthropologist and sociologist W. Lloyd Warner. See his The Family of God (New Haven: Yale University Press, 1961).

[5]Thus, Stanley Hauerwas is correct to identify the weakness of the church as a significant threat to the family. A Community of Character (South Bend, IN: University of Notre Dame Press, 1981), p. 168.

[6]This theory of sacred space is drawn from Belden C. Lane, Sacred Landscapes (New York: Paulist Press, 1988).

[7]James M. Gustafson, Ethics from a Theocentric Perspective, Vol. II: Ethics and Theology (Chicago: The University of Chicago Press, 1984), pp. 145, 160.

[8]Quoted by Robert Bellah, Beyond Belief (New York: Harper and Row, 1970), p. 140.

[9]See ibid, pp. 20-50. It is important to note that Bellah's influential scheme is not a simple evolutionary theory but a neo-evolutionary one. It is not "progressive" in the sense that more recent is always better. It does not claim that God evolves, but only that religion as a symbol system appears to. It allows for the fact that theological criteria for assessing different religious beliefs may exist; it simply doesn't provide them. And it does not argue that the four phases are airtight.

[10]Quoted in S. M. Barrett, ed., Geronimo: His Own Story (New York: Ballantine Books, 1971), p. 77.

[11]John Scanzoni, "Family: Crisis or Change?" The Christian Century (August 12-19, 1981), pp. 794-799.

[12]In another book, he labels this the "progressive" view of the family: Shaping Tomorrow's Family: Theory and Policy for the 21st Century (Newbury Park, CA: Sage Publications, 1983).

[13]The movement of the "office into the home" through computer technology may begin to reverse this pattern for some sectors of certain industries.

[14]Carl Degler, At Odds: Women and the Family in America from the Revolution to the Present (New York: Oxford University Press, 1980), Ch. 1. In Marriage and Morals (New York: Liveright, 1929; 1957), Bertrand Russell argued that this decay in family strength actually has been going on for millenia in the West, particularly among urban and seafaring classes, and in our century has almost completely eliminated the power of the father. See Chs. 3, 13-15.

[15]For a definitive account of this change of attitude, see Philippe Ariès, Centuries of Childhood, trans. by R. Boldick (New York: Vintage, 1962).

[16]Degler, At Odds, p. 472.

[17]For an incisive critique of this dark side of religion, see Karl Barth's analysis of "our attempt to justify and sanctify ourselves before a capricious arbitrary picture of God." Church Dogmatics, I/2 (New York: Charles Scribner's Sons, 1956), pp. 280-324.

[18]Though there is a spectrum of opinions on marriage and family questions among Roman Catholics and among Protestants, some fundamental differences hold. See James B. Nelson, Between Two Gardens (New York: The Pilgrim Press, 1983), pp. 59-73. For an analytically rigorous account of wider (though often complementary) differences in these two ethical traditions, see James M. Gustafson, Protestant and Roman Catholic Ethics (Chicago: University of Chicago Press, 1978), esp. Ch. 1.

[19]Hauerwas, A Community of Character, p. 165.

Chapter Two

THE CULTS SEND A WARNING

"O foolish Galatians! Who has bewitched you . . . ?
Did you receive the Spirit by works of the law,
or by hearing with faith?"

GALATIANS 3:1-2

Heresy has its uses. Its challenge to orthodoxy, as Augustine once said, presents orthodox believers with a wonderful opportunity to state their side of the argument with renewed force. And when Christian heresy takes social form, as in a number of modern "cults," it can reveal the <u>anxieties of ordinary people uninhibited by the constraints of orthodoxy</u>. The beliefs and practices of two major heterodox Christian groups in America today reflect profound dissatisfaction with modern family life.

The Holy Family of Rev. Moon

"My life has been changed," he said to me, and it soon became obvious that it had. Sitting comfortably in my living room, the Public Relations Director of the most notorious of modern religious movements slowly sipped his orange juice. He was a so-called "Moonie," a member of the Unification Church of South Korean evangelist and industrialist Sun Myung Moon. We talked long into the night; and it was only some hours into our conversation when I realized that what made this movement tick----a group whose eventual aim is to transform the entire world, every economy, every government, every society----is its aggressive restatement of the ancient claims of family over against Western individualism. In Rev. Moon's vision, the family is resacralized with a vengeance.

Moon received this vision, my new friend told me, at age 16 in Korea. Christ appeared to him and commissioned him to restore the kingdom of God on earth. After surviving imprisonment by the North Korean communists, Moon formally began his church in 1954 as the Holy Spirit Association for the Unification of World Christianity. The movement's main scripture, The Divine Principle, contains a rather complex but coherent theology which interprets the Old and New Testaments in light of Moon's revelations.

Unificationist missionaries first arrived in the United States from Korea in 1959. But the movement didn't begin to grow here until 1971, the year Moon himself first visited the United States. When disillusionment was setting in following the failure of social movements of the 1960's to remake a more just society on a solely political basis. The message of "millennial" religious groups, such as Moon's, were beginning to gain a hearing.

"Our deepest problems go back to the Garden of Eden," explained my Unificationist friend. "There God created Adam and Eve who were to form a sinless family of father, mother and children----a type of Trinity, based upon God. They had everything they needed: the knowledge, the power, the responsibility. And they blew it. Eve allowed herself to be seduced by Satan (the snake), and then later tried to cover her sin by seducing Adam. From then on, instead of God-centered families, we've had flawed families wracked by evil. This was the 'fall of man'."

"The very essence of history is a series of unsuccessful attempts to do right what God intended Adam and Eve to do," he continued. "Noah, Abraham, Jacob, Moses----they all tried and failed. As the New Testament shows, the last great attempt was Jesus Christ----who is our Savior spiritually, because he achieved spiritual salvation for us through his sacrificial death on the cross." Didn't Christ do what God wanted? "The Jews blocked him. History is not pre-determined. Despite his best efforts, Jesus couldn't prevent the Israelites from prematurely killing him before he could complete his mission, i.e., before he could become the second Adam' by marrying and beginning the ideal family." My friend's eyes flashed. "This part of Christ's mission was postponed until the Second Coming."

Moon's movement is classified as millennial because he teaches that the millennium or "last days" are our days, that the opportunity to usher in the kingdom of God is at hand. This gives Unificationists an intensity and excitement rarely seen among believers of any kind these days. "We believe this century presents us with another opportunity to restore the kingdom," he continued, "for Christ is coming again. He's going to unite world religions and put an end to the vicious chain of war, poverty, inequality and misery. The proof that this person is the Messiah will be the founding of a perfect family, a model for the world and the fulfillment of God's original intention for Adam and Eve."

The testimony of this young convert painted a different picture than that of popular press reports on the Unification Church----reports that focus on the mass wedding ceremonies, the charges of "brainwashing," and the like.[1] Sensationalist accounts rarely provide a high road to understanding. On the contrary, what drives the movement is clearly the hunger for a sacred family.

To new members, Moon and his wife are designated as True Spiritual Parents, and other members as "brothers" and "sisters." Their first job is to learn to love others spiritually, which means entering a three year period of celibacy during which they are to suppress all physical desires and pursue only spiritual goals. Only after this capacity for spiritual affection has been developed can the initiates turn to forming their own families, since spiritual love is the premise upon which God-centered marriages are to be founded.

Marriage is referred to as a "blessing" and is considered a sacrament within the Unification Church. In his role as True Spiritual Parent, Moon will often match individuals for marriage based upon his spiritual insight; in any case, his approval is necessary for blessings to occur. Most members have had their marriages blessed in large scale ceremonies over which Moon has personally presided. In one such ceremony in 1982, for example, over 2000 couples were blessed in Madison Square Garden in New York City.

Their interpretation of Scripture is shaped by family anxieties and concerns. The central problem of history for them turns out to be a family problem. The prime goal of history is the reconstitution of the family. When the God-centered family is finally established and growing, it will lead to the transformation of unjust economics, tyrannical governments, and fractured societies. The hand that rocks the cradle correctly will eventually change the world.

The Eternal Family of the Mormons

Seeing them in person, you can't miss it. A few months ago, I joined a group of students on their first visit to a Mormon church just north of our little town of Holland in Southwest Michigan. The trip turned out to be a revelation. After three hours of their sacrament service, Sunday School and various priesthood meetings, we all came away with the same conviction. Though every Christian denomination offers religious and social programs for family members such as youth clubs, women's groups and men's clubs, we couldn't think of one that comes close to matching the Mormon organizations. The Church of Jesus

Christ of Latter-day Saints (their formal name) is the American family religion
par excellence.

In addition to their elaborate church programming----which includes singing,
crafts, and sports as well as Bible study and mission training----the Mormons
surround all their members with an extensive church welfare system. It works
like an extended family. When in difficulty, any Mormon in good standing can
usually count on receiving substantial church help in the form of food, cash,
clothing, and even assistance in finding a job. Begun in 1936, this welfare
network now includes some 600 church farms, canneries, storehouses, etc.

As with the Unification Church, the family-centeredness of the Mormons has
had a decisive impact on their view of God and the sacraments. Most ceremonies
in Mormon temples are designed to benefit dead family members. Mormons
spend many hours a year searching out their genealogies, because they believe
they can perform proxy baptisms for ancestors who have passed away. In the
Mormon faith, marriage is not just "'til death do us part," but for eternity.[2]

The Mormons stress the humanity of God to a fault. The Heavenly Father
has a body of flesh and bones. Though He has perfected Himself through the
ages to His current exalted position on earth, He was once a human being like we
are. He didn't create the world out of nothing, but organized pre-existent matter.
He has company: other gods rule other worlds. And lo and behold, the earth's
God has a wife. In consort with the divine Mother, He procreates the human
race.

The Hidden Challenge of the Cults

I am not an advocate of these new religions. Some of their beliefs are
preposterous, and much of what they demand is ridiculous. To use Paul's term
quoted at the head of the chapter, the Unification Church and the Mormons are
forms of Christianity "bewitched" into departing from biblical standards. As with
Christians in Galatia in the first century, their faith appears to have regressed or
fallen backwards into a legalistic Christianity that overemphasizes works of the
law.

But what exactly has bewitched them? The "father of lies" (John 8:44) may
be involved, to be sure, but has there been anything else? What keeps
Unificationists and Mormons from orthodox Christianity? Have social forces and
conditions played a role?

The signs are not difficult to read. Running through the beliefs and practices
of both these cults is a deep, almost primal fright about the weakness of the

modern family unit. All their various family proposals (delegitimizing "falling in love" as a basis for mate selection, making preparation for marriage serious business, making marriage eternal, and so forth) appear to have this single goal---to make marriage and family holy again, to firm up their foundation . . . or (using the sociologist's term) to sacralize the family. To be sure, their solutions are heretical. But the anxieties that drive them to such solutions teach us much about the state of affairs in modern families. At bottom, the Mormons and the Unificationists aren't all that different from the rest of us.[3]

The genuine differences may originate as much in their courage as in our orthodoxy. They are saying "No" to the weakening of the family in modern America. They place marriage and children near the center of their religious life, and they take some heat for it.

Their objection against mainline Christianity is of a piece with the gentle protest of the Hopi Indians of the American Southwest, and with the objection lodged by the archaic Luo people of Tanzania.[4] For Moonies, Mormons and these pre-modern religions of the earth, we Christians have become too other-worldly. In their view, we need much less Fall/Redemption Christianity and much more Creation-centered Christianity. They have a point. The teaching of the Bible, in this connection, is a powerful one. We need to reacquaint ourselves with the family as a sacred community in our own Scriptures.

Everyone knows that the family we encounter in the Old Testament is patriarchal; the ancient Hebrew family was constituted under the headship of the father. What everyone does not seem to know is that though the authority of the father was doubtless associated with his physical strength and with divine command, it rested operationally on the father's position as priest of the household. The Hebrew family was a little society bound together by religious observances. The father presided at the Passover, a family rite celebrated in the home (Exodus 2). The family burial place was holy ground; in the earliest documents, there is more than one echo of ancestor worship. The so-called "household gods" of Genesis 31 and I Samuel 19 were probably symbols or images of (doubtless male) ancestors. The cluster of family religious observances was passed on by the father to his eldest son.

Since the strength of the Israelite family was grounded in religion, it soon became nothing less than a sacred duty to secure its continuance. To have numerous progeny was the universal wish throughout ancient Israel. Children are considered to be a heritage from the Lord, and happy is the man who has his quiver full of them (Ps. 127:3-5). Both husbands and wives feared barrenness. Rachel's deeply felt cry to Jacob----"Give me children or I shall die" (Genesis 30:1)----is representative. If a wife did not produce a son, it became the husband's sacred duty to take a second wife or concubine.   And if he died without a male heir, it was an act of piety on his brother's part to marry his widow and raise up children in his place (Deuteronomy 25:5-6).

Finally, the Hebrew family was not complete without the guest or "stranger." This could be any person separated from his kindred for some reason, and who then placed himself under Israelite protection.   He would be eligible to be included in the sacred bond in an Israelite family.   Once again, since God was the great protector of sojourners and strangers (Ps. 146:9), hospitality to strangers was grounded ultimately in religion.   "You shall not wrong a stranger or oppress him," God says to Israel, "for you were strangers in the land of Egypt" (Exodus 22:21).

The point is pushed even further in the New Testament where every family in the universe is considered to be (potentially, at least) a "little church."   This claim about the family derives from Paul in his stunning letter to the Ephesians. There is no family anywhere, including heaven, that is not rooted in God (Ephesians 3:15).   So all sons and daughters are created in an image larger than that of their parents or society.   The bond of love between parents and children finds its ultimate blueprint in God's love for human children, a blueprint crystalized in the sacrificial life Jesus lived among us (Ephesians 5:1-2).   Both parental discipline and the obedience of children are to be "in the Lord" (Ephesians 6:1-4).   Perhaps the greatest mystery associated with family life is the marital relationship, a sacred bond intended to reflect that singular love, faithfulness and communion manifest in the relation between Christ and the church (Ephesians 5:31-32).

Each family, then, is sacred in a theological sense, a church in microcosm. Motherhood and fatherhood are callings as holy, as high, as potent in their consequences as that of any priest or minister.   In fact, when it comes to teaching that worldly distinctions and honors don't matter ultimately, that all are loved equally in the kingdom of God, faithful families may teach this lesson better than any church.   The least we can say is that by renouncing competition in the midst of a brutally competitive world, homes join churches as crucial laboratory experiments in building God's kingdom.   It is the clear teaching of Jesus that the pagan way of seeking honors and distinctions is to be renounced: "It shall not be so among you" (Matthew 20:26).   When Paul speaks of the final irrelevance of perhaps the most offensive of worldly distinctions, i.e., between slaves and masters, he sets up his address with a discussion of the love and submission one to another in Christian homes (Ephesians 5:21-6:9).   As the Jewish tradition has long recognized, families can be more sacred than churches or synagogues.

The true challenge the cults put to Christian churches is this: do orthodox Christians believe in and act on what the Scriptures teach? Do we display the convictions we should possess about children and family life, or simply blend into the landscape? If Christians in America really stood up for their beliefs about the family and children, we would, as one writer has put it, "stand out like Lubavitcher Jews in Brooklyn, or Amish farmers in Pennsylvania, or Hare Krishna youngsters in the airports, or Jehovah's Witnesses ringing the doorbell."[5]

NOTES

[1]A perceptive exposé of the bias in this reporting can be found in John T. Biermans, The Odyssey of New Religious Movement (Lewiston, N.Y.: Edwin Mellen, 1986).

[2]Never mind that Salt Lake City, the Church's headquarters, has one of the highest divorce rates in the nation! It should be noted, however, that both the marriage rate and the birth rate in the Mormon community still far exceeds the national average. William J. Whalen, Minority Religions in America rev. ed., (New York: Alba House, 1981), p. 97.

[3]Adequate evaluation of cults awaits increased attention to the societal forces that give rise to them. See Florence Kaslow and Marvin B. Sussman, eds., Cults and the Family (New York: Haworth Press, 1982).

[4]Michael C. Kirwen has written a splendid description of the challenge posed to Christianity by the East African Luo people, a tribe with a one-world cosmology and a profound belief in the sacredness of procreation: The Missionary and the Diviner (Maryknoll, N.Y.: Orbis Books, 1987). Nothing translates this challenge theologically any better or more pungently than the Creation-centered spirituality movement led by the prolific Dominican Matthew Fox. See his Original Blessing: A Primer in Creation Spirituality (Santa Fe, N.M.: Bear and Company, 1983).

[5]James T. Burtchaell, For Better, For Worse (New York: Paulist Press, 1985), p. 83.

Chapter Three

A FAMILY THAT HURTS CHILDREN

"Discipline your children while there is hope;
do not set your heart on their destruction."
PROVERBS 19:18 (NRSV)

The Christian community owes a profound debt of gratitude to James Dobson, Ph.D. Through a wide variety of media over the last twenty years, he has attacked that pretense to "objectivity" so common among family specialists in our scientific age. One must focus with care on his principles rather than on the often troubling social impact of his movement. Not only is Dobson's position explicitly grounded in biblical teaching, but he has successfully exposed the hidden costs of permissiveness in American homes. Those costs are borne by children. His work provides confused and often guilty parents with an island of common sense amidst the battering surf of conflicting theories of child-rearing.

This chapter attempts to refine a number of Dobson's insights, and place them in a somewhat wider context. Trained as a psychologist, Dobson reads the history of indulgent American families too narrowly as a response to developing ideas in the discipline of psychology----in particular, to these ideas as popularized during the 1960's.[1] In fact, the roots of this problem are both more ancient and more firmly embedded in the structure of American society than the politically conservative Dobson is inclined to believe. Permissiveness has been the open secret of American families for over a century.

Down With Hierarchy

For about ten years, my wife and I have been attending a family discussion group made up originally of five and then four couples. All of us have what an outsider would call "good families," and we often remind each other how lucky we actually are. There are problems, of course. Of the many anxieties we parents have revealed to each other over the years, the most persistent one is about conflict and differences between the generations. We joke a lot about marital battles, but not so much about arguments with our children. We tend to view the struggle between the generations as an evil, conflicts between brothers and sisters as a sign of bad upbringing, and so on. Some of us worry that we are too distant from our children, that we don't include them enough.

Alexis de Tocqueville would feel right at home. Over a hundred and fifty years ago, before becoming a famous politician and an even more famous social philosopher, the Frenchmen Tocqueville visited the United States, studied its customs and institutions, and penned a portrait of the democratic family so penetrating that it anticipates the concerns of American parents even today.[2] In his book, Tocqueville celebrated the advantages of the democratic family over its more hierarchical, European version, and we can certainly agree. What we should be careful not to affirm is a deformed descendent of the democratic family, the "indulgent family," a structure now drawing fire from the Dobson movement.

The family Dobson opposes is an over-politicized family under the conditions of modern democracy. It is poisoned by an unbiblical and distinctly modern individualism. Instead of being a school for a new and possible adulthood, the indulgent family is a refuge from adulthood. Tocqueville's portrait is an excellent place to begin our analysis, since in his sketch we can see the uniqueness and political shape of its foundation.

In America, he writes, the old Roman and aristocratic family pattern has been changed almost beyond recognition. Its remaining traces can be found in the first few years following the birth of children, when of necessity the father exercises a domestic dictatorship over his progeny. But as soon as young Americans enter adolescence, the reins of filial obedience slacken drastically. The son takes charge of himself; he is responsible for his own behavior.

Surprisingly, the transition takes place without a struggle. Independence is granted freely. The father has long anticipated the moment when his authority would come to an end; he abdicates without a fuss. The adolescent knows that liberty is his right, and betrays none of the dark, disorderly passions that often disturb young adults many years after they shake off an established yoke.

In this new family, the father is more a consultant to than an authority over his children. The power he exercises is like that naturally given to any kind, experienced old man. His orders may be resisted, but his advice is usually taken. Gone is the deferential, ceremonial address to the distant father; in fact, Tocqueville finds no recognized formula in America for addressing one's father. But when children talk to their father, as they do constantly, he senses a new warmth and a certain tang of freedom.

Relations between siblings have changed as well. In the aristocratic family, children were by no means equal to each other. Because he inherited most of the family property and almost all the rights, the eldest son was chief among his brothers. To be sure, he usually protected and promoted them, since the general reputation of the house reflected credit on him. The younger sons in turn normally tried to help the eldest, since his stature as potential family head increased his ability to help them. Though hierarchal, then, the aristocratic family was at the same time an organic unit, at least in the obvious sense that the interests of all the members for the most part coincided. Whether their hearts were in harmony is another matter.

Under democratic laws, on the other hand, children have equal status. Since each child is treated with the same care, the frank intimacy of childhood easily develops among them. There is no enforced subordination to cause jealousy. As with relations between fathers and sons, so also relations between children become more intimate and gentle.

In his sketch, Tocqueville goes to some lengths to stress a point often missed by psychologists like Dobson. It is the chief lesson to be learned from sociologists of the family, to wit, that no family can be understood apart from the social factor. This new family did not "drop from heaven," but reflects the social and political conditions in which we find it.

What are those conditions? The central one is equality. When conditions are very unequal and this inequality tends to be permanent, the conception of superiority permeates the imagination of the public. In such a situation, it does not matter whether parental prerogatives are written into law or not, because custom and public opinion will supply them. The head of the family will always seem higher (and his inferiors lower) in aristocracies than in democracies.

But where conditions are generally equal and differences that do exist are not permanent, the general conception of superiority becomes markedly weaker and

more difficult to define. Again, custom proves to be more powerful than law.
When habit and necessity bring people in factories or in families together to work
in the same place or to communicate with each other frequently, it would be silly
for a legislator to put those who obey in a position of great inferiority to those
who give orders. In a democracy, customs "level," bringing these two groups
more and more on the same plane.

When people are concerned with the past more than the present, with what
their ancestors thought more than with thinking for themselves, then the parent
is the natural point of access through which to encounter ancient traditions. The
parent is the link where past and present meet. So in aristocracies, the father is
not only the family head but also the interpreter of tradition and custom. He is
heard with deference, respect and not a little fear, for the functioning of the entire
society is based on his pre-eminence and skill.

When a society becomes democratic, this whole pattern shifts. The heart of
democratic societies is the principle that it is good and right to judge everything
for oneself. Tradition shrinks in importance. Beliefs from the past provide
information more than an eternal set of rules. In such a setting, the conventions
of parental power predictably lose their force. Legally as well as practically,
fathers have less and less authority over their sons. A new kind of equity reigns
around the domestic hearth.

Prophetic though it is, this Tocquevillian portrait of the American family is
marked by a signal limitation: sociological bias. The claim that every family is
shaped by its society is accurate, but it is quite another thing to imply that the
family is merely a function of a particular social order, which is the way it
appears in Tocqueville's work. For him, the family is a dependent variable most
all the time----its own society in miniature. From our perspective, such a view
of the family can be likened to a drug or opiate, in that it wildly underestimates
the family's power over against both individuals within it and the society around
it. Dobson, happily, refuses to be drugged.

On the other hand, Tocqueville's crucial insight----society's impact on the
family----must not be lost. The family has been and remains a dependent variable
some of the time. Social change has prompted and continues to prompt a number
of changes in the family. This is easy to see with respect to those parenting
practices Dobson identifies as permissive, because extra-familial inducements to
indulgence and toward a certain "softening" of the family structure have
permeated American culture for some time.

As noted above in Chapter 1, the change began 150 years ago. The great
movements of urbanization and industrialization, the growth of bureaucratic

nation-states and the increased specialization of the workplace have combined to create a quite different setting for families today than that facing the nineteenth-century American family that Tocqueville knew. The most dramatic shift, particularly with regard to the lives of women, has been the separation of the domestic arena from the realm of productive work. Following in its train has come the so-called "loss of family function." The three traditional functions of family (work, childrearing, and education) have all become more professionalized and increasingly located outside the home.

Community support for family life has been slowly disappearing from the American scene, and the primary change agent has been our economic system. Since capital concentrations began determining the location of employment in America, we have greatly increased our mobility. This, in turn, has undermined traditional patterns of support created by the nearby relatives and community cohesiveness. Unemployment----the result of the specialization of labor together with technological advances----has made it impossible for many families to meet their own needs and secure the economic base necessary for a decent life.

Paralleling these trends is the most disturbing development of all for the American family----our culture's dual preoccupation with materialistic consumption and with the hedonistic gratification of self. Since our transition in the 1960's from a production to a consumption economy, American advertisers have been busy creating a virtually endless series of needs to be gratified. The use of sex in advertising is now commonplace. On almost any page of Cosmopolitan, Penthouse, Rolling Stone, and even Ms., sexy women and virile men look out at you and suggest that your erotic fantasies can be fulfilled NOW if you wear the right bra, smoke the right cigarette, or drive the right sports car. Instant credit with a little plastic card, instant sex with Jordache jeans. The cult of self-worship has never been more conspicuous. As the old ideals of living for others, commitment and self-restraint fade, a new god and a new social form arise. The god is Me/Myself; its most important institutional beachhead by far is the indulgent family.

Ostrich Nurture

It only looks benign. The most destructive aspect of this deformed descendent of the democratic family is the care it pretends to provide for its children. In a wonderful turn of the phrase, Horace Bushnell called this counterfeit care "ostrich nurture."[3] The ostrich, you will recall, is a gangly bird that provides us with a natural type of all unmotherhood. Instead of incubating her eggs, she deposits them on the sand to be heated by the sun. Once hatched, her young are left on their own. They go forth unattended. Bushnell knows, of course, that few if any human mothers would willingly cease the bodily care and

feeding of their own children.   With regard to nurture of the mind and heart,
however, it is a different story.

Even in Christian families, practices have been adopted and opinions go
unchallenged that make Christian parenting virtually impossible, and leave
children to a kind of nurture in the sands. The first time I saw it, I could hardly
believe my eyes. The mother (we'll call her Mrs. Smith) had just put her four-
year-old son, Walter, down for an afternoon nap, and he was having none of it.
He began to yell and scream so everyone in the house could hear him, unnerving
Mrs. Smith in the process. When he demanded a toy from the next room, and
she got it for him, he then demanded something else. When she stood up to him,
Walter simply increased his volume, and she gave in.   So young Walter
accomplished two objectives that afternoon: he did not lose his mother's
attention, and took her away from her friends.

On leaving her living room, my first thought was that Mrs. Smith was just
having a bad day, or perhaps it was only that she had one hellion of a kid. The
truth turned out to be otherwise. Her behavior that afternoon was based on a
modern, carefully worked out theory of parenting according to which all conflict
between children and their parents is classified as either a difference in viewpoint
or misunderstanding. The good parent, therefore, resolves conflict exclusively
through patience, tolerance and discussion.[4] Parental impulses in the direction
of disciplining the young are repressed, intentionally so. Children are likened to
flowers; the heart of parenting here is basically to get out of the way, to avoid
oppressing the liberty of the young, to let them grow.

There's more to the story. For Mrs. Smith, the near universal practice of
inducting children into the beliefs of their parents had become questionable; she
saw it as a major mistake, a type of brainwashing and indoctrination. Let
children discover their own principles, think their own thoughts. On occasion,
if they do fall into bad practices (as flowers, incidentally, do not), then let them
correct themselves. Parental "discipline" is usually a power trip, anyway, and
can leave permanent scars on its little targets. Unhampered by artificial external
restrictions, each child will grow up as a genuine, open-minded, original and
beautiful soul.[5]

Bushnell has Mrs. Smith in his sights. As his clever phrase suggests, the
core of this indulgent approach to parenting blends individualism with naturalism.
The faith in freedom and in human nature, particularly in young human nature,
is here virtually complete. We can imagine an ostrich mother reasoning that
since her eggs are without doubt the eggs of an ostrich, they will all produce
genuine ostriches and nothing else. So human beings are encouraged to reason

that their children will grow up, when left to themselves, into the most authentic of human types.

Teenagers love this parenting philosophy, or at least they think they do. Sixteen-year-old Laura, for example, is argumentative and very strong-willed. Every skirmish with her parents is potentially a war. Whenever her father is unsure about one of her requests to go to a party or on a trip, he says "No;" but in the debate that follows, he always backs down. He's a patsy. Why? Because his initial "No" actually means "Maybe, I want time to think about it." And when he thinks about it, his anxiety about curtailing Laura's liberty undermines his resolve every time.

We can all sympathize with this father, because the appeal of ostrich logic rests precisely on the real and almost universal difficulty of human parenting. For most of us, raising a child is the single most complicated and demanding job we're ever asked to do. The application of loving discipline to a young child---- let alone a teenager----is a complex act. Ostrich logic is made to order for parents who sense (correctly) the enormity of the task before them, and are looking for a way out. Though it often calls itself "liberal" and "enlightened" and "progressive," ostrich nurture is actually none of these things. It is a dodge, pure and simple----sloth dressed up in modern democratic theory.

The Biblical Corrective

The Book of Proverbs is wiser and more realistic, particularly about freedom in families. Its central contention is that freedom is perilous, a truth accessible to any teenager in the world in a quiet moment. Because free agency entails danger, the Proverbs instruct parents to get across to their children what the Living Refuge has told them, i.e., what they actually believe is right (morals) and true (faith) about life. Shaping children through discipline in light of holy principles and laws can be done unwisely and abused, of course, but abuse does not contravene right use. No other technique grants children the weapons to fight not only their own sin but the damage inflicted by their parents. Once discovered, the adoption of this approach has momentous significance; for the Bible is surely correct that denying such protection to your own child is to "set your heart on his destruction" (Prov. 19:18).

Destructive though it is in modern America, the family that hurts children has a perfect pose: "We're not indulgent, we're simply more democratic." The charade usually works because no faith is more fundamental for Americans than their faith in democracy. If the family is democratic, so much the better; and the more democratic it is, the better it is.[6] We Americans provide no exception to the virtually universal tendency to idealize one's own political arrangements.

So when Tocqueville gives us a somewhat lofty "democratic" portrait of ourselves, we are all too ready to believe him. When Professors Brigette and Peter Berger announce that the foundation of modern democracies is the middle-class family, we rally to its support. When Dr. Thomas Gordon tells us that the secret to effective parenting is more equality and more freedom, it strikes us as simple common sense. When Professor Michael Novak says that democratic capitalism is based on and fosters strong families, our tendency is to believe him.[7]

But it ain't necessarily so. Not everything that looks democratic is good for kids. As long as our cultural provincialism remains in place, the indulgent family is safe. In home after home, behind a smokescreen of "freedom" and "independence" can lurk ostrich nurture and betrayal of the parental vocation. Democracy is such a powerful ideology that the cultural and social "shock" of the Bible, a pre-democratic book, can help wake us up. Using the alien cultural world of Scripture, we can reflect more self-critically on our own.

Nothing in Scripture should lead us to expect a cozy fit between the family and the modern democratic state.[8]   On the contrary, we can see a persistent conflict between families and political communities throughout history. The state has repeatedly attempted to control the family by subordinating it to the polis---- an impulse recorded dramatically for us in Plato's community of wives.[9] The family, for its part, has resisted politicization. The depth and permanence of this antagonism is doubtless one reason for the fascination Antigone has generated in the Western imagination for over two millenia. The famous Greek play centers on the clash between a family and a king over burial rights.

When contemporary theorists bemoan how weak and "nuclear' the family has become, and how much it needs outside expertise and intervention, we have the same old conflict in a form attuned to the modern welfare state.[10]   There are numerous cases today where intervention by family professionals is justified. But the alleged "weakness" of modern families proves to be a difficult claim to pin down (see Chapter 1). Weak in relation to what? How is family strength and weakness being defined? Once defined, is such familial strength and weakness subject to precise and reasonably adequate measurement?

Instructed by the New Testament, a better approach is to assume a more or less permanent tension between the family and every state, and then ask whether Jesus's recorded suspicion of the family means that Christianity, in this struggle, sides with the state. Our position here is that it does not.

Conclusion

Two counter-indulgent principles in Scripture deserve special mention. In the first place, the Bible places tremendous emphasis on the family as a school. "Train up a child in the way he should go, and when he is old he will not depart from it" (Prov. 22:6). Central is the assumption that little children are profoundly receptive to the teaching of their guardians, good or bad. Applying ostrich logic to our species would be lunacy, for mistakes in the early years can prove very costly indeed. If you want your children to be unselfish and truthful, teach it. If it is desirable that our children be kind and appreciative, we'll have to teach them. If we want good decisions from our kids, we must show them---- and give them room to practice. Since most human behavior is learned, simple heredity doesn't get us very far. And children will learn what they are taught.

Secondly, the Bible teaches that all homes need a "respect trip-wire" which, when touched, sets off an alarm every child can hear. When parents discipline their child, perhaps the most important decision they make is whether or not the behavior in question constitutes a direct challenge to their authority. Is the behavior <u>disrespectful</u> as well as disobedient, or simply disobedient? If the former, the parental response should be swift and firm, leaving the child in no doubt that a structure essential to family life has been violated, to wit, the hierarchy of parents and their children.

To be sure, respect should go both ways. In Ephesians 6:4, fathers are warned against provoking their children to anger. But in the biblical perspective, parents are invested with an authority children do not possess. Scripture stresses this because homes need hierarchy (or what Dobson calls "loving leadership"), and children need to know that it is there. The rub comes when parents begin to realize that this marvelous position God has granted them is a burden in disguise. For to be effective, parents must earn their authority in the eyes of their own children. Parental authority (<u>not</u> authoritarianism) often appears as a power trip or unethical oppression, but is neither.[11] Confusion on this point is usually the beginning of the slide toward indulgent parenting.

The basic problem in this family that hurts children is the refusal to grow up. We sometimes forget that God designed the family structure itself to help all of us do just that. The system would probably cure even indulgent parents, but they leave it too soon. If you stick at parenting long enough, children will almost inevitably force you into maturity. The family is an effective school for children, we have said; and so it is. It is also a <u>school for adults,</u> a place where kids raise parents. Just as the family prepares children for service in the world, so also its fathers and mothers. "If a man does not know how to manage his own household," wrote St. Paul, "how can he care for God's church?" (I Timothy 3:5).

NOTES

[1]James Dobson, Dare to Discipline (New York: Bantam, 1977), pp. 94ff.

[2]Alexis de Tocqueville, Democracy in America Lawrence trans. (London: Fontana, 1968), pp. 756-762. We might note that he attends here almost exclusively to male family members.

[3]Horace Bushnell, Christian Nurture (London: Richard R. Dickenson, 1899), pp. 40-55. Bushnell derives his image from Lamentations 4:3, where amidst religious and familial disintegration, the Israelites are accused of becoming "cruel, like ostriches in the wilderness."

[4]The notion of the family as an institution dedicated to the happiness of its several members, particularly of its children, is a relatively recent one. Its birth appears to coincide with the beginning of the industrial era. In her essay, "The Crisis in Education," Hannah Arendt is particularly clear about the novelty of the idea that there is a special and allegedly autonomous "world of the child," a world which should attenuate the authority of all adults-- particularly teachers and parents: Between Past and Future (Cleveland: Meridian, 1963), pp. 173-196.

[5]The Scottish educational genius A.S. Neill, in his book Summerhill: A Radical Approach to Childrearing (New York: Holt, 1960), provides perhaps the best known and purest example of the philosophy of indulgent parenting. The healthy side of the book is its counter-authoritarianism, which may have been prompted by excessively legalistic parenting practices in a culture shaped by followers of a great religious figure known for his stress on law: John Calvin.

[6]For the transformation of our conception of family effected by the individualistic ethos of democratic capitalism, see Christopher Lasch's Haven in a Heartless World (New York: Basic Books, 1977) and The Culture of Narcissism (New York: Norton, 1979).

[7]See Brigitte and Peter Berger, The War Over the Family (Garden City, N.Y.: Doubleday 1983), Thomas Gordon, Parent Effectiveness Training (New York: New American Library, 1975) and Michael Novak, The Spirit of Democratic Capitalism (New York: Simon and Schuster, 1982).

[8]I know of no one more perceptive concerning the boundary between liberal-democratic and Christian assumptions about the family than Stanley Hauerwas. See his A Community of Character, pp. 72-86, 158-166.

[9]Introduced by Plato as if it were a digression, the discussion appears in the Appendix of Part II of The Republic, Cornford trans. (New York: Oxford University Press, 1945).

[10]For an intriguing analysis of the hidden control of the French family exerted by medical professionals in France, a modern democracy, see Jacques Danzelot, The Policing of Families, R. Hurley, trans. (New York: Pantheon, 1979).

[11]See Dobson's critique of Parent Effectiveness Training on this point in The Strong-Willed Child (Wheaton, Illinois: Tyndale House, 1978), pp. 167ff.

Chapter Four

A FAMILY THAT HURTS WIVES

*"The first sexual division comes about when nurture is
made the exclusive concern of women. This cannot
happen until a society becomes industrial; in hunting
and gathering and in agricultural societies, men are of
necessity also involved in nurture. "*
W. BERRY[1]

Anyone interested in that wound peculiar to so many modern women need
go no further than the spectacular work of British author Virginia Woolf. Her
view on the subject is summarized conveniently for us in two brief stories----one
about Shakespeare and the other about herself.[2]

When asked why history reveals so few female geniuses, Woolf replied by
introducing Shakespeare's sister.   For the sake of argument, she writes, assume
that there was a woman in Shakespeare's day with Shakespeare's potential, e.g.,
his wonderfully gifted sister. Compare the two siblings. Since their mother was
an heiress, Shakespeare himself probably went to grammar school, where he
learned logic and Latin, and read Ovid and Virgil. He was a wild boy who
hunted in the forest, then got married and had a child a bit sooner than he should
have. The escapade drove him to seek his fortune in London. He began hanging
around the theater district and soon became a successful actor, meeting talented
people, practicing his art on stage and in the streets, even gaining access to the
palace of the queen. Then he began to write. . . .

But what about his hypothetical sister, a girl just as adventurous and brainy
and energetic as he was? What options would face her? In the first place, she
would remain at home. She would not be sent to school; she has no chance to

be taught grammar and logic. She would have begun domestic work almost before she was out of the nursery and would then have been held to it by the all-but-irresistable authority of parents, law and custom. She might pick up a book now and then, probably one of her brother's, and read a few pages. What stood against her----and to a degree, still stands against women, particularly outside the West----were practically all the basic conditions of her life . . . in sum, her "family."

For a highly gifted girl like Shakespeare's sister, her most fundamental handicap would be lack of space. Before she was out of her teens, she would be betrothed to the son of a neighboring wool-stapler, an arrangement not easy to either delay or unravel. A trip to London is out of the question, she is told, because a woman should never travel alone. If, driven by her gift, she escapes one night, letting herself down from her window by a rope, and takes the road to London and forces her way into the presence of actor-managers in a theater, the men would laugh in her face. She couldn't become an actress, for no training in the craft would be available to her. The little woman, still pubescent possibly, must be interested in something else, they think. And so it would go. Such a girl certainly might have gone crazy or killed herself: the world's door was shut and locked from the inside.

Woolf's other story is about a gift that changed her own life. In 1918, her aunt died accidentally while riding a horse in Bombay. Aunt Mary's will specified that her niece, Virginia, was to receive five hundred pounds from her aunt's estate each year until death. Before her aunt died, Woolf had had no independent sources of income. She did odd jobs for newspapers, read to women's literary clubs, made artificial flowers, taught kindergarten, and so forth. The work was not work she wanted to do; and like Shakespeare's sister, the writing she did want to do was pushed to the margins by lack of time and space. She became resentful and bitter, particularly concerning her male supervisors, yet also fearful, even fawning, towards these same people because the economic stakes were too great to run risks.

Aunt Mary's gift changed everything. Though it didn't make her rich, Woolf began receiving the material support that any freedom worthy of the name requires: a secure income, and a room of her own. The fear, the bitterness, the slave mentality began to dissipate.

No force in the world can take from me my five hundred pounds . . . I need not hate any man; he cannot hurt me. So imperceptibly I found myself adopting a new attitude towards the other half of the human race. It was absurd to blame any class or any sex, as a whole. Great bodies of people are never responsible for what they do. They are driven by instincts which are not within their control. They too, the patriarchs, the professors, had endless difficulties, terrible drawbacks to contend with. Their education had been in some ways as faulty as my own. It had bred in them defects as great. True, they had money and power, but only at the cost of harboring in their breasts an eagle, a vulture, forever tearing the liver out and plucking at the lungs----the instinct for possession, the rage for acquisition which drives them to desire other people's fields and goods perpetually; to make frontiers and flags; battleships and poison gas; to offer up their own lives and their children's lives.[3]

American women today, of course, are not as cramped by their families as would have been true in Shakespeare's time. Most homes are better off financially. Menial domestic tasks have been sharply reduced by nineteenth and twentieth century technology. As we've seen, the family is generally more democratic. Reliable, inexpensive birth control techniques have been developed recently, giving couples a new measure of control over reproduction.

But two features of modern family life in combination threaten to arrest the gains Western women have made over the last four hundred years. The first is the hallowed privacy and "domesticity" of the middle-class family, the sharp division between the realm of family care and the sphere of "productive" work (i.e., labor for which one receives a wage). Since the industrial revolution, productive work has been progressively taken out of the household; what was once both a productive and a consanguineal unit is now increasingly conjugal (see Chapter 1). The second characteristic is the intensified focus on children in American families, and----since Dad is usually away in "his world" most of the day----on the mother-child relationship.[4]

The Feminist Critique

The great protest against this state of affairs is contemporary feminism. The literature of the women's movement is so rich and penetrating that no one examining the family today can afford to disregard it.[5] This same literature is complex enough to make generalizations about it somewhat hazardous. Nevertheless, here are two of them:

1) Feminism strengthens Christian teaching on the family. A signal contribution of feminism to Christian social analysis is its exposure of male tyranny and female sloth in modern families. Evidence of sin in marital relations is, of course, not surprising, but feminist criticism here is often brilliant and prophetic. Feminists have shown, for instance, how biblical concepts such as "servanthood" and "selflessness" and "sacrifice," intended as gender-blind

principles, tend in practice to be transformed into feminine ideals and applied chiefly to women. They have encouraged Christian women, faced with such tendencies, to ask "Why?" and "Says who?"

Feminism has also helped Christianity see the ways middle-class family life can diminish and trivialize the calling of God in the lives of modern women. The doctrine of divine vocation requires each Christian to see her special gifts as a calling from God to serve and obey God. Shakespeare's sister might have a better fate today, but the poignancy of Woolf's tale about this hypothetical female derives from the fact that she would not be out of the woods yet. In some respects, middle-class norms of femininity and women's role have narrowed since Shakespeare's time, and often don't approach the breadth of the biblical ideal in Proverbs 31:10-31.

2) Feminism recovers ancient Greek insight into the family. If the value of feminism for Christianity rested only in such refinement of biblical discernment, this would certainly be enough. But it does more. Feminists have recaptured a sense of the profound human significance of political activity and of the unique "space of appearance" (i.e., space to appear as a unique person) it furnishes.[6] They then apply this discovery, derived from ancient Greek sources, to a class of people the Greeks themselves excluded from public life: women.

When Plato and Aristotle subordinated the domestic sphere to the public sphere, they had a very clear reason for doing so. They considered the household to be a sphere of necessity, not of freedom. Its distinctive trait is that people are driven there by their wants and needs. Typical family activities----eating, giving birth, dying, cleaning, cooking, harvesting, marketing----revolve around keeping the body alive, perpetuating the species, continuing communal life, and so forth. The Greeks were not denying its importance. Without domestic activity, politics would not be possible. They insisted, rather, that the activities and satisfactions of the two spheres were different. The family was pre-political. To enter politics is precisely to free oneself from the family, i.e., from the necessities of life and the relationships they originate. By remaining tied to domestic duties, the Greeks argued, women excluded themselves from public life.

As a result, their humanity was diminished. For Socrates, Plato, and Aristotle, some sort of participation in the polis (public life) was the summit of human fulfillment. They saw what was grand and honorable in the public sphere, and as a result demoted all other spheres in relation to it.

We can detect an echo of this demotion of the domestic sphere in contemporary feminism. This is not a biblical argument. But are feminists nonetheless correct in their perception of a justified hunger for "action" and for

"space of appearance" among women under modern social conditions? I believe
they are.

The Biblical Critique

The tradition of criticizing the family for its self-centeredness and favoritism
is an ancient one. It appears in the New Testament. Before and after the
beginning of the Christian era, it has marked doctrines of monastic orders,
religious sects and certain social philosophers. Modern feminism updates the
tradition by using Marxism and the social sciences to look beneath comforting,
pious descriptions of "hearth and home" to the reality of modern child-centered
family life.[7] In a "pro-family" culture such as the United States in the 1990's,
feminist anti-familism has become almost essential to keep one's balance. It
might remind Christians of an even deeper critique of the family in the Bible
itself.

"If anyone comes to me and does not hate his own father and mother and
wife and children and brothers and sisters...," said Jesus, "he cannot be my
disciple" (Luke 14:26). The searchlight thrown by the New Testament on the
family is relentless, often startling, and on occasion difficult to understand. Yet
its "harsh sayings," such as this one, supply exactly the advice parents and their
children need to hear----particularly women trained to believe that child-bearing
is their irreversible vocation by nature, and that once children arrive, their roles
as citizen, wife, colleague, and so forth, should take a back seat to their role as
mother. For child-centered families, the Bible is a strange world indeed. Let us
see how.

When a family becomes committed to Christ and instructed by Scripture, a
quiet revolution begins. The domestic and private "spheres" surrounding most
contemporary women change their character. In the Bible there is hardly a trace
of the view, reflecting modern middle-class social conditions, that the woman's
natural place is in the private sphere while the man's place is in public. The New
Testament does attend to the domestic sphere, and sometimes its references are
gender-specific in ways that reflect this. The "weaker sex" may use her inner
beauty to win unconverted husbands to Christ (I Peter 3), the birth of children
may have salvific significance for the bearer (I Timothy 2), and so forth. But the
central thrust of the Greek argument, with its subordination of the domestic to the
political sphere along with the parallel tendency to idealize public life, evaporates.

Jesus' own obliviousness to this distinction between private and public is
revealed nicely in the famous story of Mary and Martha (Luke 10:38-42), where
the male Jesus does important "public" work in Martha's "private" household.
When Mary, Martha's sister, chooses to listen rather than help with domestic

duties, Martha complains to Jesus.   She has much serving to do, and Mary
should darn well help.   But Mary is right, Jesus replies, not because domestic
duties are degrading, but because when compared with listening to Jesus, they are
not the "better part" for Mary. Martha could have seen this herself, were not her
judgment clouded by anxiety and worry.   The private/public distinction is
irrelevant.

So biblical thought refuses to either insulate or subordinate the family in
society as a whole.   Within this framework, the Bible stresses a distinction
internal to the family which is fundamental to the argument of this book.   The
biblical distinction calls for a seismic shift in family practice, for it entails a
change in the relationship between the two fundamental axes----the parental and
the spousal----by which the family is structured.[8]

Within every family, Scripture teaches, the most primary and permanent
bond is not between parents and children but between husband and wife.   In
Genesis 2:18-23, the coming together of man and woman is presented as God's
intention in Creation and as the fulfillment of their need for companionship.
Children are not mentioned. In that imperative for family which reaches the level
of the Ten Commandments, children are told to honor their father and mother
(Exodus 20:12), not vice versa.   In Genesis 2:24, the cleaving of a man to his
wife is shown to be a union of such permanence that even family ties are
loosened on its behalf.

The primacy and prominence of the marriage bond within family life
becomes even more explicit in the New Testament, where almost every reference
to family turns out to be a discussion of the relation between Christian husbands
and wives----not between Christian parents and children. It is Christian marriage
that must "be held in honor by all;" the marital bedroom, rather than the
household per se, is charged with remaining "undefiled" (Hebrews 13:4).
Referring to the Hebraic view of God as the husband of Israel, Jesus compares
His own mission to a wedding (Mark 2). It is the Christian marriage relationship
in which Paul sees a close analogy to the mystical bond between Christ and His
church (Ephesians 5).

As any candid mother or father will confess, the right balance between
marital and parental roles is a difficult one to maintain. For this reason, while
the teaching that non-marital relations should be subordinate to the marital bond
may seem obvious to parents today, it is not trivial. Its liberating message is
directed particularly to women who have known the overpowering, stifling
presence a family can be.

Here we come face to face with exquisite biblical insight into the provisionality of the family. By "provisional," I mean the family is voluntary (it is not necessary) and fallen (it is not perfect). "To the unmarried and the widows I say that it is well for them to remain single as I do," wrote St. Paul, in words that echo from the first century into our own (I Corinthians 7:8). Being married and having a family is neither higher nor lower than being single and not having a family, because both are vocations, callings. Both are voluntary. Both are intended to serve Christ and His community in the world.

Also, the family is fallen. The fact that the sacred relationship between parent and child is more natural (and less voluntary) than the marital one does not make it more innocent. The more indispensable an institution is, the more alert we must be when it claims too much for itself. There are times when the family needs nothing more deeply than to be put in its place. When a woman wanted to exalt Jesus' family with the words, "Blessed is the womb that bore you, and the breasts that you sucked," Jesus brusquely replied: "Blessed rather are those who hear the word of God and keep it" (Luke 11:27-28).

Marriage Transformed by Christ

The secret to resisting the child-centered family can be put simply: keep marriage primary. "Keeping the romance in marriage" is not exactly my meaning here, but it is close. In Matthew 19:3-9, Jesus makes a surprising claim about the sexual and emotional bond between husband and wife. It has a depth and permanence, he says, that the spouses themselves may not notice. God has been active in their joining (v.6), and even "from the beginning" (v.4) created their gender differences with this union in mind. The only parallel bond would be the faith relationship to Christ Himself.

The implications of the astonishing exaltation of marriage in the Bible is nowhere more evident than in I Peter 2-3. With the coming of Christ, the Greek subordination of domestic to political encounters gives way under pressure from a new kind of community, whose leader calls its members "out of darkness into His marvelous light. Once you were no people but now you are God's people" (I Peter 2:9-10). Whether free citizens (2:13-17) or slaves (2:18-20) or wives (3:1-6) or husbands (3:7) or victims of persecution (3:13-22) or simply ordinary members of the community (3:8-12), any word or deed of these early Christians that "witnesses" or gives an "account . . . (of) . . . the hope that is in you" (3:15) assumes precisely the primacy Aristotle reserved for political action. The question of location or sphere loses its decisiveness. In Christ, the region between husband and wife provides a space of appearance on par with civic, economic, and more broadly social relationships.

Both the testimony of Peter in this passage and of Paul in Ephesians 5:21-33 is that Christian marriage is now a site for action in this transformed sense.[9] The basis of the idea is probably the first Creation story, cited by Jesus in Matthew 19:5----"Male and female he created them" (Genesis 1:27). In contrast to the second Creation story (Genesis 2:4-24) where God creates man (Adam) in the singular, in the first chapter of Genesis humankind originates as plural, different beings. The distinction in no sense implies inequality, a first and a second, a higher and a lower, an original and a derivative. Men and women speak and act to show themselves as unique human beings; each makes his or her appearance in the human world like no one else who has ever lived, testing the words and deeds of others. "Iron sharpens iron, and one person sharpens another" (Proverbs 27:17). The original form of this condition is the encounter of male and female (first Creation story), an encounter which culminates in the marital relationship (second Creation story).

Yet the classical Greek view of marriage and family, updated by feminism, has descriptive importance. If we look at the actual state of our homes, there is indeed a tension between marital and parental roles. To a great degree, the family is still the realm of necessity. By encouraging husbands to center their lives outside the home and wives to focus on a narrow "domesticity" within it, the modern child-centered family does diminish the humanity of its occupants, particularly the lives of women.

Efforts to change domestic spaces within industrial societies, even when not broadly successful, are revealing. Melusina Pierce and Charlotte Gilman, for instance, led a remarkable group of "material feminists" who campaigned to de-privatize domestic work in the United States in the nineteenth century. Women are deeply wounded, they argued, by their economic dependency and by the physical separation of household space from public space. They started housewives' cooperatives that would undertake housework for payment. They developed plans for kitchenless houses, and popularized the idea of collective kitchens, laundries and child care centers to remove these tasks from the private home. They pushed architects and town planners to look at the effect of design on family life.[10]

Feasible or not, such experiments indicate that modern child-centered family patterns may be exacting a heavy human toll. The cost is high in the Christian community; for as Paul argues, the family is to be a training ground for Christian leadership. Any aspirant to the office of bishop "must manage his own household well, keeping his children submissive and respectful in every way; for if a man does not know how to manage his own household, how can he care for God's church?" (I Tim. 3:4-5).

The parallel was clear, in Paul's view, between managing one's household and caring for God's church. But is the modern Christian family helping wives or hurting them? Aren't too many of their lives so diminished by the isolation of their families, plus the subordination of marital to parental roles within them, that the family is less a training ground than a dead end?

For Christians, however, the best remedy for child-centeredness is not the classic feminist one of attacking traditional families. This is because the problem does not reside in the traditional family per se. Most traditional families are structured with husbands as the head, and clearly assign the roles of both husband and wife. In egalitarian families, gender roles are flexible with each partner asserting their growth needs, and then working toward consensus or compromise. The Bible permits both models; the Gospel can be lived out in either and distorted in both.[11]

Rather, the most effective antidote to this family that hurts women is to get husbands and wives to listen more deeply to the New Testament, in particular to Christ's call to wives to be out ahead of their husbands. Child-centered families where wives find themselves "beneath" their spouses in any worldly sense have missed the Gospel message twice over. They have turned away not only from the magnificent Christian principle of equality in marriage (Ephesians 5:21; Galatians 3:28), but also from the command that Christian wives take the initiative in training their husbands for the kingdom of God.

I refer here to Christ's puzzling message, mediated through Paul's and Peter's writing, that Christian wives submit themselves to their husbands. "Wives, be subject to your husbands . . ." (Ephesians 5:22). "The head of a woman is her husband," Paul writes in I Corinthians 11:3. "Likewise you wives, be submissive to your husbands" (I Peter 3:1). By detractors and supporters alike, these passages are widely and mistakenly interpreted as law.[12] They are not. They have nothing directly to do with family structure. Their purpose was certainly never to identify the place of wives and women on the organization chart of modern households. On the contrary, these passages define a starting point for a new way of peace, a way depending not on the weaknesses of women but on their strength.

Though unintelligible both to the ancient Greeks and to moderns who misread Christian marriage as a purely private affair, the aim of these subordinationist passages is public (as well as private) transformation of a quite radical sort.[13] They appeal to a uniquely female sense of agency exposed by Christian revelation in a marital context.[14] Throughout the New Testament, the calling to "submit" is to teach Christ. This submission is Christic; this submission is training to change the world.

The Ephesians and I Peter passages commending the subordination of Christian wives are of particular interest, because with appropriate gravity and directness, they both appeal to the wife as a person. This appeal was without parallel in first-century Greek and Jewish literature. Christian wives are not being told to follow their husband's orders; they are being asked to decide for themselves. They are being asked to consider a course of action which----apart from the "love of enemies" tradition so visible in Jesus' life----few if any wives would choose to follow.

In a fashion both stirring and baffling to the world, Paul and Peter appeal to Christian wives to consider putting down their weapons first. Because of the risk involved, it is a decision no one should make for anyone else. No matter who the husband is, it is a job requiring flexibility, savvy, and a good deal of moral strength. For twenty centuries after these words were written, the world that surrounds and shapes families remains a violent place. The modern nation-state, for example, convinces most of us to either kill or pay for the killing of people we have never met, for reasons with which many of us may disagree, in the cause of interests we rarely understand.

In a marital context, the form of wifely non-violence will vary with the situation, just as it does in society as a whole.[15] On occasion, the form will be simply non-resistance or witnessing to the truth while enduring suffering if necessary. Sometimes the form will be passive resistance or refusal to comply with unjust expectations. In passive resistance, the power comes from the capacity not to participate in an objectionable practice, and may be aided by organizing with others----frequently with women. A third form would be more assertive and could be called direct intervention. Still, the aim is not to harm but to convert one's husband or "enemy." Initiating a marital separation would be an example of non-violent direct intervention.

But whatever form this "submission" takes, the aim is to follow Christ and change the world. The world-transforming character of wifely subordination is clearest in I Peter 2-3, where it is placed explicitly alongside economic and political subordination (2:13-20). As Ephesians 5:21 implies, the fact that Paul calls Christian wives to submission first does not mean that he didn't want husbands as well as wives to submit to one another "as to the Lord." Rather, his thinking probably paralleled the reasoning of the traditionalist Hindu Gandhi, for whom women were the incarnation of ahimsa (non-violence) and in spiritual matters usually the stronger of the two genders. Or from the angle of the second Creation story, the great Jewish convert was doubtless suggesting that women are the crown and culmination of Creation, the logical ones to address first regarding this essential and difficult practice within the way of Christ.

NOTES

[1]Wendell Berry, The Unsettling of America (San Francisco, CA: Sierra Club Books, 1977), p. 113. There may be no greater--though largely hidden-- cost of the Industrial Revolution than its wholesale diminishment of the natural nurturing roles of men.

[2]Virginia Woolf, A Room of One's Own (New York: Harcourt, Brace and World, 1929; reprinted at Harvest/HJB Book, 1957), Chs. 2-3.

[3]Woolf, A Room, pp. 28-29.

[4]Edward Shorter, The Making of the Modern Family (New York: Basic Books, 1977).

[5]Books by feminists and about feminism number in the thousands. A helpful history, identifying both the movement's Christian and non-Christian sources and types, is by Olive Banks: Faces of Feminism (Oxford: Basil Blackwell, 1985). In contemporary American feminism, the definitive exposé of the child-centered family of the post-World War II years was Betty Friedan's The Feminine Mystique (New York: Norton, 1963). On the costs of denying women their space of appearance in the Christian community, see Joyce Erickson, "Let Us Now Praise Women: Telling the Story Whole," The Reformed Journal (May, 1986), pp. 6-11. Both Erickson and I read Aristotle through the extraordinary eyes of Hannah Arendt. See Arendt's The Human Condition (New York: Doubleday, 1959), pp. 23-45.

[6]The phrase is Hannah Arendt's. The analysis here is indebted to her The Human Condition, pp. 155-190.

[7]Within a society as nervous about its families as the contemporary United States, the family-negative streak in feminist writing is usually qualified and restrained. Not so on the movement's often creative fringes, where a work of Mary Daly may serve as an intellectually startling and representative example: Pure Lust: Elemental Feminist Philosophy (Boston: Beacon Press, 1984).

[8]This is what Stan Hauerwas means when he writes that Christianity is a "threat to the family" when it breaks the natural necessity of family by "setting the institutional form necessary to make marriage voluntary." Community of Character, p. 174. He needs to mention that the Hebrew Scriptures are also a threat.

[9]In a short but profound book, the contrast between the Christian exaltation of marital love under God (agape) and the Greek ideal of civic friendship (philia) is explored by Gilbert Meilaender in Friendship: A Study in Theological Ethics (Notre Dame: University of Notre Dame Press, 1981). C.S. Lewis covers similar territory in his classic, The Four Loves (New York: Harcourt, Brace and World, 1960).

[10]See Delores Hayden, The Grand Domestic Revolution (Boston: MIT Press, 1981).

[11]Though many Christians believe otherwise, the Bible contains no single pattern for family or even marital life. Marriage and family customs change within the Bible, as they have continued to change throughout history. What Scripture provides is less a prescribed ancient pattern for families than a set of profound resources for discussing how God's will can be lived out in our own families here and now. See Diana S. Richmond-Garland and David E. Garland, Beyond Companionship: Christians in Marriage (Philadelphia: Westminster Press, 1986). For a lucid and comprehensive argument that there is a single pattern for marriage and family in Scripture, see Steven B. Clark, Man and Woman in Christ (Ann Arbor: Servant, 1980). I disagree with Clark on a number of fronts, but he is a gifted, practical theologian. The attention he gives to the Creation stories is instructive, and his massive study will alert any interested reader to the issues at stake in the area.

[12]For an exceptionally clear example of this tendency, see the wildly popular Christian Living in the Home (Grand Rapids: Baker, 1972) by Jay E. Adams.

[13]The biblical scholarship underlying this position has been summarized and shaped in a masterful way by John Howard Yoder in his The Politics of Jesus (Grand Rapids: Eerdmans, 1972), particularly Chapter 9.

[14]For empirical evidence, from the discipline of psychology, of a uniquely female sense of agency, see Carol Gilligan, In a Different Voice: Psychological Theory and Women's Development (Cambridge: Harward University Press, 1982).

[15]The tactical complexity of Christian non-violence is stressed in The Universe Bends Toward Justice, ed. by Angie O'Gorman (Phildelphia, PA: New Society Publishers, 1990).

Chapter Five

A FAMILY THAT HURTS
HUSBANDS AND GRANDPARENTS

*"If our children are to flower, we need to sow them
well and to nurture them . . . and direct them toward
the highest light, to stand straight and tall----that they
may take our place as we took that of those who
planted us and made way for us, so that in time they,
too, may make way and plant. But if they are truly to
flower, we must go to seed; we must wither and give
ground. "*

L. KASS[1]

The United States is sitting on a moral time bomb. Due to advances in
nutrition and medicine, the number of older people in our society is expanding
rapidly. Our second fastest growing population group is comprised of the nearly
seven million Americans eighty years of age and over----a group which is likely
to double in size by the year 2050, when it will become the fastest growing
segment of our population. Our society is growing older so fast that the median
age of U.S. citizens, which was thirty in 1980, will jump to thirty five by 1995.
And yet, of the estimated six million aged Americans in need of some type of
home care, only a puny fraction of them receive it.

It is time we looked at elderly persons (and at our attitudes toward them)
more carefully. In parts of Asia and Africa today, particularly where belief in
an afterlife has remained firm, the elderly are considered a vital source of
richness and strength in a society. Those in life's final stage are thought to be
so close to the life beyond and its spiritual power that they appear as virtual
repositories of the sacred. Though never without flaws, they appear to reach a
kind of perfection: a wisdom and dedication to the divine can radiate from their
very being. As a result, the aged are accorded a position of enormous respect
and honor, because they can be and do things that only the old can do----as
judicious arbitrators, as educators of the young, as natural saints.

To Western eyes, such a state of affairs appears at once archaic, mildly superstitious, and vaguely appealing. Since the Industrial Revolution, the status of the aged has been changing. As a rule, we have become less oriented toward the past; we may venerate our ancestors to varying degrees, but we certainly don't worship them. Most historians conclude that particularly in contemporary America with its cult of youth, the position of the elderly has declined.

But again, we should beware of over-simplification. There is little use in pretending to know more than social historians do about the extent, the speed and even the direction of this change.[2] Since historians are suspicious, we too should be wary of theories that make all pre-modern, non-industrial societies into a "golden place" or a "golden age" for the old. On closer inspection, these traditional societies prove to be not as uniformly well-disposed toward their aged population as we once thought.

We need also to beware of an equally fragile theory which turns the nuclear family into a demon----blaming it and industrialism for the destruction of the extended family network, through which allegedly the old exercised their power and gained their security. It is now common knowledge that the nuclear household has been the dominant family form not only since the rise of industry, but in pre-industrial Western societies as well.[3] Thus the notion that because of its structure, the nuclear family somehow impoverishes the elderly today is, by and large, a myth lacking firm support.

In and of itself, the nuclear family is no demon. But dissatisfaction with the "small" and "isolated" family of today is far from whining and idle chatter. The thesis of this chapter is that a deformation unique to modern family life----a "closed" family that hurts fathers, husbands and grandparents----is indeed demonic and needs to be resisted. The closed family is a complex pattern of work and family structure that develops in response to the rapid social change characteristic of industrial societies. Its central feature is the destruction of the bonds of family life across the generations. Before identifying some strategies for changing it, we need to examine the character and causes of the closed family.

Families in Union Park

Since he visited Chicago repeatedly as a boy, it was only natural for Richard Sennett to become fascinated with the Windy City as a subject of research. After training at Harvard, he decided to focus on patterns of family life and work experience in an area called Union Park, part of Chicago's near West Side, during the years 1872-1890. His study, published in 1970, turns out to have more than simply historical significance. It is the finest analysis of the closed family in print.[4] Sennett discovered that under certain conditions, the nuclear family retreats into itself, destroying first the bond between father and son, and more generally undermining the capacity of children to deal effectively with the changing world around them.

This peculiar type of family has four main characteristics: intensification, insulation, specialization and father weakness. Many modern nuclear families are marked by an intensity that does not appear to have been at all common before the industrial era. Though "private" in the sense of being separate from the surrounding community, there is a distinct communality and lack of privacy within the family group itself. The family becomes intensified and even inflated to the point that it appears as not only a special world, but the world itself in microcosm. Family members begin to believe that everything important in social relations can be experienced within the bounds of the home.

In a unique way, the closed family is also insulated. One parent, usually the father, represents the family in the work world at large; all other family members stay out of it. The mother either does not work, or works part-time "for economic reasons." The children are trained for more than a decade in schools, and enter the work world only at the end of adolescence, if then. Unlike family life in the medieval era, where the period in which children were considered helpless and in need of special nurture tended to be much shorter (until age seven or eight), modern families inherit the idea of a period of helplessness extending at least until late adolescence. The head of the household is expected to protect this "haven in a heartless world," while the wife and children live somewhat apart from the world and its manifold temptations.

Among Union Park families, Sennett found that the burden of this insulation falls first on children, particularly on the sons. Far from constituting an environment in which children can train to function in the adult world, it actually created a barrier making it more difficult to deal with that world. The period of alleged "helplessness" was over-extended, and became a chronic condition. Intense, closed families impoverished the emotional and moral life of their children by depriving them----too completely and for too long a time----of direct experience with the complex extra-familial world of adults.

A third mark of the closed family is its specialization, a feature which reflects the increasing complexity and functional specialization of the surrounding industrial world. The organization of modern families (with their work-world person, nurturant person, and helpless persons-in-training) echoes a social order in which the division of labor is a dominant theme. Where schooling has become compulsory, what used to be a crucial job for families is turned over to "specialists," i.e., public school teachers.

As the specialization of work escalates in modern societies, the <u>site</u> of jobs is not determined by the location of the family but by capital concentrations and organizational efficiency. Hence the fabled mobility of modern family units. The work is not expected to go where the family is; the family is expected to go where the work is, even more so (and more often) as families search for a larger and larger piece of the monetary pie. Mobility has been a prime cause of that alleged erosion of access and allegiance to relatives of nuclear families today. We will return to this point later in the chapter.

Sennett's most stunning observation is the fourth and last mark of the closed family: <u>father weakness</u>. In his survey of nuclear families in Union Park within a limited historical period, Sennett uncovered a puzzle. While most of Union Park's families showed strong characteristics of intensity, some didn't. Most were highly private and insulated, but some weren't. In the same time period and in the same place, under generally similar conditions, he asked himself, what factor might explain the difference between these two family types?

Sennett found his answer in, of all places, literature and labor statistics. When American literary artists portrayed the lives of those migrating to industrial cities in the late nineteenth century, their characters experienced both excitement and a profound sense of uncertainty, fear and dislocation. Images of dread tended to predominate. As a bulwark against this new and alien world, young adult male immigrants often married and founded a family quickly. On occasion, the first girl they seriously dated would become their wife. The dislocation was so extreme that some region of safety and emotional security had to be established.[5]

The families established by these men were "intense" in precisely the sense described above. Experiences outside the family tended to be impersonal, disjointed and fragmented; inside the family was a quite different world of intimacy and direct personal contact. The family became a retreat amidst chaos; for the new urban migrant, it was quite often his <u>only</u> sanctuary. Beneath the surface joy and intensity of these families lurked the husband's fear and uncertainty.

In one sense, there is no question that the families of these men were "strong." The strange and tumultuous conditions of urban life did not break these institutions down or even change them. On the contrary, the usual pattern was for the young to repeat the domestic situation of their elders, and do it as soon as they could. There was never much time between breaking away from home and marriage. Like their fathers, the sons tended to marry early and re-establish the same type of family setting.

At the heart of this intense, closed family is the weakened position of the father. As literary portraits of the home show newly aggressive mothers and docile fathers, so labor statistics reveal that the job pattern of fathers from intense families was at best static and occasionally one of decline. They were going nowhere. Union Park fathers in less intense families, on the other hand, showed a generally upward trend toward white-collar status in the labor force. As a rule, the families of these fathers were less sheltered, more work-oriented.

It is no wonder, then, that closed family fathers were perceived as "weak" or even "absent" by their sons. His half-failure at work, his immobility in a world where mobility and acquisition are the hallmarks of success, led to his failure as a father as well. His greatest gift to his children would have been to prepare them to meet the world successfully; but his entire pattern of life testifies that Dad himself has not been able to do this. We can assume, plausibly, that such fathers presented a defensive picture of the work world to their children----full of dire warnings about the pitfalls of the industrial world, the dangers of stepping out of line, and so forth. The guidance these fathers provided was not in terms of meeting the world but fleeing from it to the intimacy and security of the home . . . exactly as they did a generation earlier.[6] The advice has less and less relevance to working sons, who cease looking to Father for guidance in the outer world.

An apathetic pall falls over Father's family role, for in truth he is little more the master at home than in the outside world. He may play at "patriarchy" for awhile and fool the younger children; but Mother usually understands the closed family game in all its tragic poignancy. What began as a retreat into the family ends in the destruction of family across the generations as men seeking security in the home become increasingly weak and passive within its bounds.

The genesis of the closed family, then, is the fear of chaos and disorder in response to a social upheaval----such as the transition from urban migration to Union Park homes, or the movement from an experience of the Depression and World War II to neat suburban split-level houses.   Wherever it takes root, the impact of this family pattern is to weaken the mutuality between the generations----with Dad typically as the first casualty. The emotional rapport between fathers and sons, the continual advice-giving and advice-taking that once held the two generations together, turns increasingly vague and vacuous. The father becomes less and less a positive force in his children's lives.

The Chief Victims

The other victims, of course, are the grandparents. By distancing itself from its own elderly, the overly-nuclear closed family co-operates with a pervasive disease in American culture concerning old age and death.[7] By ensuring that the aged and dying rarely live among us, the closed family can easily become the very structural expression of this disease. Might the fear of chaos and disorder on the one hand, and the fear of death on the other, be two sides of the same coin?

Part of the American problem, to be sure, stems from changes of relatively recent date. Because of modern medical technology and sanitation techniques, the number of deaths at an early age has declined sharply. As the average life span increases, separate communities for the elderly----such as nursing homes and retirement communities----have been growing. Greater geographical mobility has meant that most of us live at some distance from aged and dying relatives, including our parents. As a result, Americans are becoming inexperienced with the reality of death.

We are also profoundly uneasy about it. We deny death at every available opportunity. Notice how our language is filled with euphemisms such as "losing" Aunt Edie, Grandpa "passing away", the possibility of something "happening to" me, and so forth. How rarely we hear: "When I die. . . ." We transform graveyards into "memorial gardens," a corpse into "the remains." In the presence of a dying or grieving person, notice how difficult it is to know what to say. The death and dying movement has helped many, but has not had much effect on American life as a whole. Even Christian funerals can be hurried affairs, filled with denial, giving such disembodied attention to the afterlife that the reality of death, loss and grief is left largely unacknowledged.

Such an attitude is radically at variance with Scripture. The Judeo-Christian tradition has consistently emphasized not only attentiveness to the aged but also the importance of a clear awareness of one's own death. "Teach us to number our days that we may get a heart of wisdom" (Psalms 90:12). Leviticus 19:32 reads, "You shall rise up before the hoary head, and honor the face of an old man."

In an atmosphere filled with so much denial and pretense, it is no wonder modern Americans have difficulty relating to the dying, to the grieving and even to Grandma and Grandpa. Our denial has two sides, and both deserve some attention. We close out our elderly first by romanticizing the "Golden Years" and denying the losses and weakness of aging, and second by denying what biblical and other ancient cultures seem to know intuitively----that old age is a source of power needed by the rest of the community, that there are strengths and potential gains in aging.

For anyone wishing to avoid the dark side of old age, the Bible is certainly the wrong book to read. In Ecclesiastes 12, for example, there is a brutally candid and stark account of the aging process. The years are coming, the Preacher writes, when the passing of days will no longer give you pleasure (v.1). The sun and the moon and stars, which previously were bright, will become dark; and the clouds, which usually disperse after the rain, will return (v.2). In these latter days, even strong men will be bent (v.3). We will be like old grasshoppers, dragging ourselves along without desire (v.6). There will be terrors, merriment will cease (vv.4-5). This is how it will be "before the golden bowl is broken . . . and the dust returns to the earth as it was" (vv.6-7).

The Preacher is surely correct: many aspects of old age are not lovely. When best friends in the generation of an elderly person die, the loss is irreparable. When the elderly retire in our society, they often suffer a major loss in personal dignity. The community that organized and received the life contribution of these individuals is often gone. The work that gave their life much of its meaning is gone. Western society places tremendous importance on independence and self-sufficiency; and as old age progresses, this too ebbs away.

The weaknesses and losses of aging are real; they have been recognized for millenia. Though health technology qualifies them temporarily, no medical miracle can make them evaporate. What we need to recognize, though, is that this half of the story is not the most important part. There are strengths and potential gains in aging just sitting there, waiting to be acknowledged by those with eyes to see. Alongside the physiological deterioration and social withdrawal, we find among our elderly population a great rite of culmination, of progress and fulfillment. Through this ritual, the old can and do regain a childlike vitality; and by their contact with the rest of us (particularly the young), they revitalize society by renewing our capacity for feeling and candor and by heightening our sensitivity to God.

By distancing itself from its own elderly, the closed family does something quite unnatural, usually unnecessary, and always unwise. Who has not noticed the peculiar and universal affinity between the very young and the very old? No one can communicate with a youngster quite like a grandparent. No longer worried about their own children, the old are free for the young in a way that parents rarely are. The honesty and frankness of the aged can be breathtaking; it is no accident that kids love them.

Another legendary characteristic of older people is their willingness to tell stories. For some time now, gerontologists have noted that telling life stories enables the elderly to enrich their immediate lives by bringing back many, diverse memories and seeing the deepest meanings of their lives more clearly. Often not noticed is the value to young parents and children in hearing these stories (in which they are often a central character) and in being encouraged to tell their own stories. Obviously, no one can start this process or keep it going quite like a good set of grandparents.

To shut out grandparents is also to lose their wholesome sense of adult dependencies. One gain in aging is the gradual discovery that some dependencies in adult life are beneficial. Spouses discover how much they need each other; parents discover how much they need their children. Particularly in technological societies that celebrate individual freedom and mobility, the value of this discovery is difficult to overstate. For families threatened by the disintegrating toxin of individualism, there may be no better vaccine than the presence of a good grandparent!

In a word, grandparents are part of family. The command to honor your father and mother (Exodus 20:12) has no time limit. To those of us with grandparents who are a joy to have around, it comes as no surprise that this Fourth Commandment is the only one of the Ten Commandments with a promise ("that your days may be long . . .") appended. As a group, the aged may constitute the most summarily ignored source of strength in modern society. The value of each elderly person to the younger segment of their own family goes far beyond what I've enumerated here. Can a family actually be a family without them?

Four Strategies

To speak of "opening up" the closed family in America today is not unlike a call to battle. There are huge and formidable social forces conspiring to keep it closed. The denial of death, making us dis-eased around the aged, runs deep in American culture; it is subtle, and next to impossible to fight with secular weapons alone. Furthermore, many of us live with the burden of historical inertia: raised in closed families, our natural tendency is to continue the tradition as if it were the optimal family form. The unprecedented dynamism of our society continually creates incentives to retreat from disorder and make the family a bulwark against a threatening and confusing workplace.

So it is not going to be easy, but there are four strategies we can try. First, Christian churches need to recapture the ancient biblical understanding of death as the teacher of wisdom about how to live.[8] It is difficult to imagine a less popular message in contemporary America, a fact which testifies to the deeply death-denying quality of many of our lives. The wisdom tradition in the Bible places tremendous importance on imagining our own mortality. Though largely banished in our society, this theme pervaded West European culture in the Middle

Ages. Its truth remains. There is no way to avoid death without avoiding life; knowing oneself as mortal is to recover a sense of the precious fragility of life and to renew the impulse to love it. "It is better to go to the house of mourning," advises the Preacher, "than to go to the house of feasting; for this is the end of all men, and the living will lay it to heart .... The heart of the wise is in the house of mourning" (Ecclesiastes 7:2, 4).

Second, Christians in the United States need to give more attention to the political side of this problem. Is American society ordered in such a way as to give adequate support to our elderly citizens? Our national family today is too closed for comfort. At the moment, we have neither national health services nor a national home care program. The Scandinavian system, one of the most progressive in the world, pays "home helpers" who come to the homes of those older persons who live alone and assume chores the dwellers can no longer perform. With help at home, elderly persons with declining vigor need not worry about such matters as heavy housekeeping or cooking or burdensome errands, and can devote their energies to real interests such as reading or relations with neighbors, even learning new skills. Best of all, day-to-day fears and uncertainties are reduced. The Scandinavian plan also includes the option of "integrated housing," where the immediate neighbors of the elderly are often young couples with children.[9] To be sure, taxes are high in Scandinavia; but from a moral and a Christian point of view, might our taxes be artificially low?

Thirdly, closed families need to be addressed by a message with "family appeal," but which calls them to a cause beyond the family. They are too much the insulated haven, and not enough the servant open to the community. The Christian church is well situated and commanded by its Lord to announce exactly such a message: the ecclesia is itself a new, transformed family in which God is loving Father and Mother, in which love is no longer to be preferential (all are brothers and sisters), and which is called to love the whole world on behalf of the Son of God. In this particular context, the genus of the Christian message turns out to be this: it dethrones the closed family without destroying it. After learning to care for parents, siblings and offspring, Christian families are called to move from "hostility to hospitality," putting this training to work through service in the larger world.[10]

If our analysis has been correct, closed families confront the church with a special need to rebuild bridges between the family and work. By giving some attention to the largely forgotten concept of "reparenting," the church might provide some genuine assistance here. In a host of respected professions today, the key skills required are clearly a duplication of the love and care for persons necessary to be a decent parent, or reparenting. The location may be separate from family, but the most profound part of the work is familial. Some social service occupations would be one example. My own job in college teaching would be another. The Christian ministry, its counselling aspects in particular, would be yet another. And here is Scott Peck describing how the skills of family life reappear----or rather, should reappear----in psychotherapy.

> There is nothing at all inappropriate in the feelings of love that a therapist develops for his or her patient when the patient submits to the discipline of psychotherapy, cooperates in the treatment, is willing to learn from the therapist, and successfully begins to grow through the relationship. Intensive psychotherapy is in many ways a process of reparenting. It is no more inappropriate for a psychotherapist to have feelings of love for a patient than it is for a good parent to have feelings of love for a child. To the contrary, it is essential for the therapist to love a patient for the therapy to become successful, and if the therapy does become successful, then the therapeutic relationship will become a mutually loving one.[11]

As the Apostle Paul recognized in I Timothy 3:2-5, the gap between the accomplishments of family life and effective service beyond the family is not as wide as it sometimes seems. Inside and outside our professions, we meet adults with deprived children living inside them, longing for a tenderness not received from a father or a mother. To love such a person after the manner of a parent is nothing less than to minister to them as God's priest, standing in God's place as their own parents were meant----but failed----to do. Parenting outside the family is love's way to open up a closed family, turning it out toward the community. And it often provides a bridge between family and work.

A final strategy Christians might adopt is to help closed families get closer to their grandparents. Befriending older blood relatives can be tricky. All children owe respect and honor to their parents, but not worship. Paul's advice concerning "real widows" (I Timothy 5:3-16) is quite remarkable in this connection. No generalized "veneration of older women" clouds his judgment. Some widows were so self-indulgent as to be in effect dead even while they lived (v.6). Others were idlers, gossips, and busybodies (v.13). Still others were already "straying after Satan" (v.15). When deciding about economic assistance, Paul urges, the church should avoid false piety and be realistic.

The same advice could be given to adult children befriending their parents once again. Every situation is different, of course, but we all can learn from the case of Kandy Stroud.[12] A free-lance journalist, Stroud lives with her husband, her children and her 80 year-old mother in Washington, D.C. Six years ago, her mother was practically dead. After her husband died, this former public-relations consultant went into a slow decline. She continued to live in her Manhattan apartment----watching hours of TV, smoking more, drinking more. Then one Monday morning, the housekeeper found Stroud's mother lying on her bedroom floor, where she had apparently been for 36 hours. She was dehydrated, talking irrationally and in pain. Stroud rushed her by ambulance to Washington, where doctors determined that though she broke her hip, no stroke had occurred. After two weeks of hospitalization, Mother moved in with Daughter.

It was not an easy transition. Both Kandy and her mother were angry at the arrangement. Mother had refused numerous invitations to move in earlier; and though there was no real alternative, she didn't want to move in now. She had also refused to live with a companion. During her decline, the spunky matriarch had found much to criticize in Stroud's attempts to "help out."

But no matter. The years since Stroud's mother moved in have transformed the entire family. The greatest change was in the elderly patient herself, who has almost literally come back to life under the "motherly" supervision of her daughter. The first sign of her new ambition was to throw away her walker, as she began walking up and down stairs three and four times a day. She now walks to the hairdresser, goes to the symphony, and attends her grandchildren's school plays and soccer games. Her spunky Irish wit returned.

The children say they have learned patience and understanding and a concern for others. Grandma gives them total adoration, minus maternal harangues about cleaning their rooms and doing their homework. Stroud got her mother back. They have all learned that touching is a healing phenomenon. The daily hugs of a six-year-old Karate Kid, the arm of a son-in-law to escort her to the car, the embrace of her daughter all have proved to be restorative. Even the family animals seem to help: patients who nurture pets have a higher success rate than those who don't.

While the particulars of the Stroud solution are not for everyone, the lesson is universal. We never outgrow our need for regular affection and attention, i.e., for what family normally provides. This is what makes the closed family system----a pattern distancing families from their grandparents----so sad. It should not surprise us, therefore, that an incontrovertible sign of <u>Christian redemption</u> in community is that all its members are treated "like family." The Apostle Paul put it best: "Do not rebuke an older man but exhort him as you would a father; treat younger men like brothers, older women like mothers, younger women like sisters, in all purity." (I Timothy 5:1-2).

NOTES

[1]Leon R. Kass, Toward a More Natural Science, p. 316.

[2]For some provocative thinking on the question, see Beth Hess and Elizabeth Markson, eds., Growing Old in America, 3rd ed. (New Brunswick: Transaction, 1985).

[3]Brigitte and Peter Berger, The War on the Family, p. 87.

[4]Richard Sennett, Families Against the City (Cambridge: Harvard University Press, 1970).

[5]In psychological terms, the closed family is a defense against pain, a detour around social contact and diversity in experience. For an analysis of the wider social impact of this pattern, see Richard Sennett, The Uses of Disorder: Personal Identity and City Life (New York: Vintage, 1970).

[6]One source of the closed family I did not explore is employment that is itself dehumanizing and alienating. A portrait of the effect of such work on working-class families can be found in Lillian Rubin, Worlds of Pain (New York: Basic Books, 1976, pp. 155-184.

[7]See Ernest Becker's explosive The Denial of Death (New York: Free Press, 1973).

[8]See Marcus Borg's fine essay, "Death as the Teacher of Wisdom," Christian Century (February 26, 1986), pp. 203-206.

[9]Tad Szulc, "How We Can Help Ourselves Age with Dignity," Parade Magazine (May 28, 1988), pp. 4-7.

[10]The phrase is from Henri J. M. Nouwen. See his splendid Reaching Out: The Three Movements of the Spiritual Life (Garden City, NY: Doubleday and Co., 1975), Chs. 4-6. See also above, Chapter 2.

[11]M. Scott Peck, The Road Less Travelled (New York: Simon and Schuster, 1978), p. 174-175.

[12]Kandy Stroud, "I Am Mother to My Mother," Newsweek (August 4, 1986), p. 7.

Chapter Six

A FAMILY THAT HURTS THE WORLD

"A generation goes, and a generation comes,
but the earth remains forever."

ECCLESIASTES 1:4

When he wrote these words, the Preacher expected his readers to be in a position to learn from the earth, from its grandeur and its permanence. The ecosystem of a Florida swamp points to the intricacy of divine Creation and Providence. The fury of an ocean storm and the fierceness of mountain landscapes powerfully suggest divine apatheia or ("indifference") which teases us out of our petty desires, out of our preoccupation with ourselves and into God's grace.[1] The earth is a marvelous symbol of the divine.

But have we lost our ability to learn from it? For the first time in history, the majority of Western men and women do not live in direct contact with the land, with the sea, or with the many species of natural life. Increasingly, even Western farmers who do engage with the earth are not trained to live with nature, but simply to harvest from it. Our food is processed and packaged. In our daily work, most of us do not shape organic materials using skills responsive to natural properties. We don't hunt and skin animals; we don't weave flax; we don't work in wood.

On the other hand, the earth is not benefitting from this reduced human presence. Indeed, we burden the earth more now than we ever have. Topsoil is being destroyed around the world at an alarming rate--six billion tons per year in North America alone. Nuclear plant accidents and massive oil spills are becoming more common. We are in the midst of an "extinction spasm" of major proportions. Ordinarily, a species of plant or animal dies out about every 2,000 years. Currently, species are dying out at the rate of one every 25 minutes![2]

The causes of our environmental crisis today are complex. Resource consumption in developed countries is out of control, and badly needs to be reduced to reasonable levels. The same point can be made regarding explosive growth in the world's population. In the last two hundred years, the human population on this planet has quintupled, and is still growing fast. Our growth rate is such that the world must accommodate a new population roughly equivalent to that of the United States and Canada every three years.

For almost our entire history as a race, maximizing reproduction has been the measure of biological success. Threatened variously by diseases, natural disasters and human enemies, we homosapiens have followed this standard for thousands upon thousands of years. We have "succeeded" beyond our wildest dreams. Through a series of technological innovations that include farming, sanitation, and the control of many epidemic diseases, we are now in the driver's seat. We are the dominant animal on the planet by any and all measures. Biologically, this is the very definition of success.

But the dark side of our triumph now looms before us. Almost overnight, the rules of the game have been reversed, and limiting reproduction has become essential for civilization's survival. This is particularly important in the United States, where the birth of a baby imposes more than a hundred times the stress on the world's resources and environment created by as birth in a developing country such as Bangladesh. Babies in Bangladesh do not grow up to own automobiles and air-conditioners or to eat grain-fed beef. But reducing our birth rate turns out to be only a portion of Christian responsibility in this connection.

Helping Our Children

Our enemy is more subtle and pervasive than some philosophy promoting large family size. On the contrary, it is an attitude and a way of thinking that has been growing in Western culture for 400 years----ever since it received unintentional support in the Reformation (see Chapter 7). It profoundly affects our view of ourselves as families. What must be reversed in our time is the process of desacralization.[3]

By desacralization, we mean a reduction in the intensity and frequency with which a community experiences the sacred or the holy. The process of desacralization is a process of becoming less religious, of losing one's piety. Since the seventeenth century, this process has been driven by a seismic shift in the way we view the natural world. We now see this world and ourselves "scientifically." With the possible exception of the rise of Christianity itself, humankind has never experienced a perspectival transformation quite like the growth of modern science.

Through the influences of early natural scientists such as Galileo (1564-1642) and Newton (1642-1727), the world of nature began to appear more and more as an infinite machine----moved only by its own laws, and not open to any other dimension of reality. We have learned to see the "real" outside world as cold, hard, silent, and regulated throughout by mathematically computable laws.

This mechanical, desacralized view of nature has proved to be both a pre-requisite for and a consequence of the Industrial Revolution in the West. When capitalists needed natural resources for their factories or wanted to measure the value of nature in monetary terms, they were aided by the new conception of nature as a valueless, indifferent machine devoid of inherent purpose. One can easily discern an affinity between early scientific doctrine and the ideology of the rising commercial classes. So our target here is perhaps best termed the industrial-mechanical view of nature.[4]

One consequence of this new approach is that we are now more secure as we face the natural world. Historically, attitudes toward nature have been tinged with fear derived from society's vulnerability to the powers of nature. Today we fear for nature, rather than fearing nature itself. Our task today is to reposition ourselves to learn what God has to teach us through the earth.

We might start with our children, who often display a great fascination with ants, rabbits, and flowers while "wasting time" in the backyard. What can be learned from this? We adults could learn to change our rhythms if we attend to non-human life which often communicates in slower cycles. The rhythm of human communication is rapid, while learning from nature may require attention spans of an hour, a season, perhaps a lifetime.

But learning from our land and from our place is well worth the effort.[5] Such listening is different from social communication; it stretches our senses, our intuition and our imagination. Is not this that makes fishing a stream or tending a garden or hiking in the wilderness so refreshing? They exercise psychic muscles that have shrunk in our modern, computer-saturated, anthropocentric hall of mirrors.

We need consciously to affirm with our children those relationships with nature that previous generations took for granted. When you sense your child bonding to a place----a secret "fort," perhaps, a personal territory he can run to, a refuge away from home----support it. Consider living in one place for longer periods of time. Put your children in the presence of teachers who can name and explain the plants and animals in your region, who know the life cycle of an area. And learn to hear non-human voices that have never stopped speaking in our lives. Writes poet Gary Snyder:

One must learn to listen. Then the voice can be heard. The nature spirits are never dead, they are alive under our feet, over our heads, all around us, ready to speak when we are silent and centered. So what is this "voice"? Just a cry of a flicker, or coyote, or jay, or wind in a tree, or an acorn whack on a garage roof. Nothing mysterious, but now you're home.[6]

Helping Our Marriages

Resisting desacralization in our marriages means rediscovering the sacredness of the family, of the bond between parents and children, of the "household." There is a profound connection between sexuality, fertility, and the earth that Protestants in particular may need to relearn. Marriage, parenting, and the care of the earth each contain disciplines that point toward the other two, and all normally come together whenever we think of "family."

Until recently, there was no division between sexuality and fertility, of course, because none was possible. Now it is possible through modern technology and birth control in its many forms. And because it is now both possible and profitable, Americans have cut most of the cultural ties between "sex" and marriage and family. AIDS notwithstanding, sexual contact is generally "free from worry." One of the most potent and tantalizing ideals of post-industrial capitalism----unencumbered sexuality----appears to be within our grasp.

But the cost of implementing this ideal has been high, and continues to mount. The price we are paying is the breakdown of our communal life, and in particular what Wendell Berry calls "the dismemberment of the household." As the meaning of sexuality becomes less and less understood as energy properly subject to discipline and restraint, and more and more insulated from the institutions of marriage, family and household, these institutions themselves begin to disintegrate. Increasingly young people approach marriage in a state of profound confusion, having few if any plausible ideas about how to imagine or enact it. With family and the practicalities of marriage well beyond their horizon, they often can think of few reasons for sexual congress other than "liking each other's company." Liking another person may be a good reason for friendship, but certainly is not a sufficient one for marriage.

Berry is surely right about the pain and sense of rootlessness that the isolation of sexuality in our time brings in its trail:

When it is no longer allied by proximity and analogy to the nurturing disciplines that bound the household to the cycles of fertility and the seasons, life and death, then sexual love loses its symbolic and ritualistic force, its deepest solemnity and its highest joy. It loses its sense of consequence and responsibility. It becomes "autonomous," to be valued only for its own sake, therefore frivolous, therefore destructive----even of itself. Those who speak of sex as "recreation," thinking to claim for it "a new place," only acknowledge its displacement from Creation.[7]

To stop hurting the world, the first test for any marriage is the attitude of the couple toward children. Jim Burtchaell writes that "we are all meant to be godparents to the children of the world. Every youngster requires attention from dozens, even hundreds, of generous adults, and kindnesses and services beyond what his or her parents could ever provide."[8] This is the Christian vision of child-bearing. Children are sacred. We must somehow take care of our own without turning our backs on the children of others.

Not only is this vision breathtaking; it is radical. Its quality is suggested in this story of a famous feminist travelling to India, one of the world's overpopulated countries.[9] The visit was sponsored by the Family Planning Association of India, and it staggered her. She encountered exactly the opposite of what she expected.

In all the villages she entered, she never found an unwanted child. Parents loved and cherished their children for a clear reason: they had fought hard against disease and malnutrition to have them. The bearing of children gave Indian women seniority in their villages. And the seniority had real substance. The women were more important and more powerful in family affairs than were the men. Nothing could be done without them.

The feminist, on the other hand, was viewed as an unfortunate woman because she had no children. The experience led her to question her own former ideas about birth control. Americans who advocate birth control across the board for all other cultures, she concluded, don't appreciate the uniqueness of the American attitude toward sex. In the United States, sex has become an indoor sport. We imagine that sex is the primary thing. But in these villages, they hardly know how to use the word "I." It is "we" all the way. The primary relationship is family.

Perhaps even the problem of overpopulation needs to be reconceived. The feminist returned to the example of an Indian village to make her point. "The entire village had squeezed into one half of a room, and had left the other half to me. And when I looked at these people, I knew perfectly well who there were too many of. There were too many of me."

This is not to say that overpopulation is not a problem in the world today, or that birth control is unnecessary. Overpopulation is a problem, and modern methods of controlling conception do constitute a step forward. Our point is rather that the casual use of any kind of birth control is unwise, because the application of our will to fertility is always a serious, moral decision. It cuts close to the heart of the sacredness of the family.

Helping the Earth

Some folks still believe that population surplus is determined by numbers of people alone. So we continue to agree with the myth that overpopulation is driven primarily by poor people who don't know enough to limit their reproduction. This is not the case. The measure of overpopulation is the impact of people on ecosystems and on non-renewable resources. While it is true that developing countries severely tax their environments, the resource consumption in rich countries threatens the earth's capacity to sustain us all.

Happily, there is no need for despair. Today nearly all developing nations have family-planning programs in place. Some smaller countries, such as Singapore, Costa Rica, and Thailand, have already achieved substantial reductions in their birthrates. Larger countries, such as Mexico and India, have not been so successful. The world's most populous country, China, now has the world's most stringent family planning program----allowing only one child per urban couple, and two at most in rural areas.

With some certainty, we are now able to identify the social changes that tend to promote smaller families. Perhaps the most important change is to improve health and sanitation conditions, which will lower infant mortality rates on the one hand and increase life expectancy on the other. Another crucial change is to elevate the status of women or, as in the case of the Indian villages just mentioned, ensure that this status does not decline. Education for women is crucial, for women in developing countries typically apply their education to upgrading their family's health and nutrition. With their children more likely to survive, parents are more receptive to family planning.

Closer to home, there is considerable room for improvement in the safety and convenience of birth control devices, with some stress placed on education about the need for them. The United States is one of the more backward of developed nations in this connection, and it is my impression that Christian churches bear some responsibility for the situation. We pay a price of more than a million teenage pregnancies annually----of which more than half are brought to term, with 60% of them born to unwed mothers.[10] As all Christians should agree, there is too much dependence on abortion for birth control in the United States, a practice which probably could be reduced through wider availability of contraceptive information and materials.

On the earth today, a family that intentionally engages with nature, that loves its children, that limits its own size and----with sensitivity----encourages others to do so, is a family that helps the world. As a global society, our rate of growth has begun to decline slowly, but we have a long way to go. As long as our rapid expansion and over-consumption continues, the abuse of the environment will remain common, and the voice of the earth will be sad.

NOTES

[1]Belden C. Lane, "Fierce Landscapes and the Indifference of God," Christian Century (October 11, 1989), pp. 907-10.

[2]For a useful summary of the condition of the planet earth, see National Geographic (December, 1988).

[3]The best study I know of this process is by Sabino Aquaviva: The Decline of the Sacred in Industrial Society (Oxford: Basil Blackwell, 1979).

[4]So argues H. Paul Santmire in The Travail of Nature (Philadelphia, PA: Fortress Press, 1985), pp. 133-137.

[5]Geoffrey R. Lilburne's A Sense of Place (Nashville, TN: Abingdon, 1989) provides theological support for this assertion.

[6]"Good, Wild, Sacred," in Meeting the Expectations of the Land, Wes Jackson, Wendell Berry, and Bruce Colman, eds., (San Francisco, CA: North Point Press, 1984), p. 223.

[7]Wendell Berry, The Unsettling of America, p. 117.

[8]James Burtchaell, For Better, For Worse, p. 80.

⁹Cited in <u>ibid</u>, pp. 82-3.

¹⁰The rate of U.S. births to unwed mothers has quadrupled since 1960, and now accounts for almost one out of every four births in this country. This dramatic increase has taken place <u>in spite of</u> the legalization of abortion. National Research Council, <u>Risking the Future: Adolescent Sexuality, Pregnancy, and Childbearing</u> (Washington, D.C.: National Academic Press, 1987), p. 1.

Chapter Seven

FAMILY, KINGDOM AND CHURCH

"The real sin of marriage today is not adultery or lack
of 'adjustment' or 'mental cruelty'. . . . It is not the
lack of respect for the family, it is the idolization of the
family that breaks the modern family so easily, making
divorce its almost natural shadow. It is the
identification of marriage with happiness and the
refusal to accept the cross in it. "

A. SCHMEMANN[1]

As we have noticed, the New Testament does not pay much attention to the family. Its dominant interests lie elsewhere. But at the same time, its most elaborate set of instructions to family members----a mere seventeen verses near the end of Paul's letter to the Ephesians (5:21-6:4)----reveals much. The Old Testament is quoted twice (Genesis 2:24 in Ephesians 5:31; Exodus 20:12 in 6:2-3). The central theme of the passage is obedience, i.e., the submission of family members to one another "in the Lord." In a fashion almost certain to be provocative to modern sensibilities, the writer underlines his theme of obedience by moving immediately from advising husbands, wives and children to advising slaves and their masters (6:5-9).

A rather odd feature of these instructions provides the focus for this final chapter. Paul appeals to Christian family members to place the deepest realities of their life together within a new and larger context: the church. Indeed, Paul's sense of home here is that it is a little church.[2] In the Christian tradition, therefore, the royal route to a better understanding of the family has always involved a renewed sense of the mysteries of the church and of the kingdom of God. It is to these mysteries that we now turn.

The Mystery of the Kingdom

Behind the earthly union of husband and wife, Paul writes, there stands a spiritual reality that shines through it and infuses it with meaning. Individual Christians know this sacred reality primarily as a set of constraints on wives (5:22-24), husbands (5:25-28), and children (6:1-3). Paul sees all this as a great "mystery" (5:32; musterion, Gk.; sacramentum in the Vulgate translation).

Precisely what sort of mystery does Paul envision in marriage? Is the musterion marriage qua marriage? Is marriage itself the outward sign of a sacred reality? Does the act of marriage establish a connection with the redeeming power of Christ? Does the blessing of the church establish this connection? Is the marital state instituted by God to dispense grace to all who enter it? If we can answer any of these questions in the affirmative, then the mystery of marriage is of the type that all Christians find in baptism and in the eucharist, i.e., marriage should be classified as a sacrament.[3]

But I do not believe we can.[3] In the case of Ephesians 5, the Vulgate translation is misleading. For "sacrament" in its theological sense means an outward sign of a sacred reality, whereas musterion, wherever it occurs in the New Testament, refers to the sacred reality itself. When Paul says explicitly that the mystery he sees in marriage is Christ and the church (5:23b), we should take him at his word. Recalling a distinction we made in Chapter 1, to be sacred and to be Christian are two different things. Sacred though it is, marriage itself does not sanctify its participants; it does not bestow faith; it does not point unambiguously to the world's Creator, Judge and Redeemer.

On the contrary, marriage is a mystery for Paul exactly in the sense that it conceals and reveals at the same time. The mystery reveals itself to the eyes of faith, but unbelief cannot understand it. "To you has been given the secret of the kingdom of God," Jesus said to his disciples, "but for those outside everything is in parables" (Mark 4:11). Parables, in fact, are probably the best example of what the New Testament means by "mystery," because they all possess this quality of simultaneously revealing and concealing. Marriage is a parable of God. To be sure, it "bears witness" but----as any survey of (even Christian) contemporary marriages will amply confirm----in a decidedly indirect way.

In his Babylonian Captivity of the Church (1520), Martin Luther makes two further arguments we should consider. How are Christians to determine what is sacramental and what isn't? For Luther, a sacrament is a divinely instituted rite containing a word of divine promise. The best way to distinguish between real and apparent sacraments is Scripture alone; for otherwise our emotions and "priestcraft" will take over, and we will have a hundred sacraments. But

Scripture nowhere states that marriage was instituted by God to be a sign of His promise. We can see with Paul that marriage is a figure or allegory of divine things, but figures and allegories alone are not sacraments, according to Luther. The so-called "great sacrament" in Ephesians 5:32 is Christ himself, not a man and a woman.[4]

He advances this "worldly" interpretation of marriage a step further with a second argument. To elevate marriage to sacramental status would be to depreciate pre-Christian and non-Christian marriages. Marriage is part of the order of Creation that embraces all people----Israelites and heathen as well as Christians. For Luther, restricting marriage to the baptized is ecclesiastical arrogance, pure and simple. It is a form of "grasping" or sin. It makes the church an easy target of ridicule from without; for some Christian marriages are worse than heathen ones, yet we call them "sacramental" in the former case and never in the latter![5]

Luther's argument here is that marriage is a sacred gift of God to the entire world, not to Christians only. Those who think otherwise march shoulder to shoulder with those who believe that Christians have a monopoly on honest statecraft, that Christians make better businesspersons than non-Christians, and the like. In a word, those who disagree with Luther often wish to reverse that profound "letting go" of the sacred which lies near the heart of the Reformation.[6]

This Reformation impulse receives its clearest expression in Luther's doctrine of the two kingdoms.[7] Though the Reformation eventually destroyed the unity of the Western church, this was not Luther's intention. He was passionately concerned about the true unity of Christ's Body. But his study of Scripture forced him to the conclusion that the church's unity can lie only in Jesus Christ as He lives in His Word and sacrament, and not in social or political power. For Luther, there could be only one church of Christ----the kingdom of the preached Word of God. Here Christ has always ruled, not by the sword, but exclusively with His Word.

The kingdom of the world, on the other hand, though it serves the same Lord Jesus Christ, serves Him through the office of the sword by punishing evil and protecting the innocent. These two kingdoms, Luther believed, will exist together as long as the world continues. They should never be torn asunder; to be governed adequately, all human communities need both. Yet the kingdom of God and the kingdom of the world must not be mixed together either. Preaching cannot govern nations. The unity of the church cannot be effected by the sword.

In the church of Rome, Luther saw a Christian community in need of "letting go." That is to say, the church was illicitly mixing the two kingdoms, absorbing into itself parts of the world that needed now to be resecularized, i.e., released from its control. Among other things, this meant a new interpretation of marriage----removing its status as a sacrament and re-visioning it as a divine institution for the preservation and comfort of the human race. Luther wanted to make clear that though marriage is a sacred estate, one is neither justified nor sanctified by entering it. Grace and holiness come only through the merciful and sin-forgiving Word of God, i.e., through Christ.

As we have seen, the Western family today stands at the end of a four hundred year debate, initiated in the Reformation, over what the sacredness of the family means. It is of the utmost importance that we distinguish sharply between two terms in this debate----terms which, though logically distinct, are often confused with one another: secularization and desacralization. By secularization, we mean the gradual transformation of both church and society along the lines of Luther's "letting go."[8] In the church, secularization means Protestantization----reducing the number of sacraments, decentralizing ecclesiastical power, a stress on the proclamation of the Word, a rejection of the magical use of the sacred (such as veneration of the relics of saints), the simplification of worship, etc. In the world, it has meant the slow emancipation of various sectors of society previously under church control and direction----as in the revolt against absolute monarchs, the separation of church and state together with the rise of religious liberty, the liberation of education from ecclesiastical authority, and so forth.[9]

By secularization, then, we mean a fairly definite historical process with a precise beginning: the Reformation in Europe. The path this process has taken varies depending on a wide range of geographical, social, political, and economic factors that impede or encourage the process, that block parts of the process but not other parts, that color the process with local adaptations, and the like. Geographical factors often played a significant role: the relative security of Protestantism in Britain because of the Channel, for example, was crucial to the success of Protestants on that island. Certain historical events----such as the outcome of the French Revolution (1789)----had a decisive impact on the path secularization took in particular regions or cultures.[10]

In sum, secularization is a change in religion. Desacralization is a loss of religion----a reduction in the intensity and frequency with which a person or community experiences the sacred. As indicated in Chapter 1, the peculiar position of this book is that it seeks to be Protestant and Catholic at the same time. On the one hand, the secularization of the family is seen as a good thing, because Protestants are right that neither marriage nor family was ever intended to attain sacramental status. On the other hand, the Roman Catholic protest against the modern desacralization of the family in the West and against the accompanying distaste for children is also right.[11] Surely one of our crucial tasks today is to recover a sense of the sacredness of family life.

The Mystery of the Church

The sacredness and religiosity of the family put it out of step with our desacralized society. In a sense, it is a community in exile----a counter-cultural alternative to the individualistic, competitive values that infuse our modern urban world. Yet as a sacred, Edenic retreat from this world, the modern family is twice out of step. For in case after case among believing Christians today, the family tends to displace the church.

The New Testament pushes us in precisely the opposite direction, toward what might be called a "counter-displacement."[12] The religious and communal center of life is no longer to be the family but the church. It is "through the church" that the manifold wisdom of God is now to be made known to the principalities and powers (Ephesians 3:9). It is the church that is "a royal priesthood, a holy nation". . . once no people but now God's people (I Peter 2:9-10). Our primary task now is to seek and cultivate gifts that do not fragment but build up and edify the church (I Corinthians 12-14).

In I Corinthians 7, Paul spells out the implications of this counter-displacement for family life. It may be the most fascinating single passage in all of Scripture. In it, Paul goes to great lengths to distinguish between what he is conceding, what he is recommending as his considered opinion, and what has been revealed to him by Christ. It is as if he knows he is addressing a subject of the highest importance, and yet at the same time walking through a mine-field where his words can be easily misinterpreted.

The heart of his message is that the conclusion of the world's story is now in view. The Messiah has come, and with him, the beginning of the end of the world. Christ's coming means that the future----that vague, amorphous dimension of our lives----has been drastically shortened. "The appointed time has grown very short" (v. 29). "The form of this world is passing away" (v. 31). The mist has begun to evaporate; we can see.

Shortening the future naturally should have a galvanizing impact on those who see it clearly. "Let those who have wives live as though they had none, and those who mourn as though they were not mourning, and those who rejoice as though they were not rejoicing, and those who buy as though they had no goods" (vv. 29-30). Everything one does is transformed by this shortening of the present age.

The most persistently controversial of Paul's recommendations in I Corinthians 7 is his preference for the single life (vv. 1, 7-8). But his point throughout the chapter is that everything depends upon what God----in light of His Son's arrival----is calling one to do (v. 17). To be sure, marriage and family are transcended and limited by the coming of Christ, but so is celibacy. The decisive event for Paul is no longer what we do, but what Christ is doing with and for us. Note his explicit reason (v. 35) for writing this advice: "to promote good order and to secure your undivided devotion to the Lord."

So this is not exactly an attack on marriage and family, but it is a displacement of them on behalf of the church. The church itself is a family. For Christians, it becomes the First Family. Jesus tells his disciples that they may lose their families, but will receive new ones "a hundredfold now in this time" (Mark 10:29-30). The most repeated prayer in Christendom is the Family Prayer wherein believers pray to a new Father, "who art in heaven" (Matt. 6:9). The church is the "household of faith" (Galatians 6:10). The entrance to this new family, a "flock" or a community open to all the world, is the crucified Christ (John 10:1-18).

The Mystery of Faith

Wherever Christ stands against families, he is actually calling family members to a new home. The search for our true home is one of the deepest impulses in the human soul. All of us want to get there. It is a place where we know the setting and the people; but even more, it is a place where we are known. It means a place where we are freed to be ourselves, where the truth doesn't threaten us but makes us free (John 8:32). Home is the place where there will always be a place for us as a sister or brother, as an equal member of the family (Luke 15:11-32). It is where the awesome divisions between different racial types, social classes and nationalities fall away, as they did when the church was born (Acts 2:1-13). Home, finally, is a city that never declines or deteriorates; you can depend on it being there.

But how does one get to such a place? This question of questions receives theological clarification in a biblical passage warning against apostasy: "Here we have no lasting city, but we seek the city which is to come" (Hebrews 13:14). The author of Hebrews could have attacked the search for home itself, but he does not. On the contrary, communities in this world do anticipate our true home. Both the homes where we were born and the homes we build can foreshadow it. Our true city, however, is not here; for if it were, we would have found a worldly city that lasts, but they never do.[13]

In the book of Hebrews, the coming of Christ is seen as the long awaited entrance of something that lasts into our constantly changing world. "Jesus Christ is the same yesterday, today and forever" (Hebrews 13:8). He did not come alone, but rather comes surrounded by a virtual cloud of human witnesses: Abel, Noah, Abraham, Sarah, Moses, Rahab and many others (Hebrews 11). As we have seen, to follow Christ is to join a new family of that faith both pioneered and perfected by Jesus "who for the joy that was set before Him endured the cross" and now is with God (Hebrews 12:2).[14]

This is the city without end, the home that lasts. After Abel offered to God a more acceptable sacrifice than Cain, he died; "but through his faith he is still speaking" (Hebrews 11:14). In this new family is a kingdom more real than any nation or civilization. Despite appearances of fragility and weakness, its strange power in Jesus has "overcome the world" (John 16:33). Even now, the coming city lives----not in speech alone or in deeds alone, but in faith alone.

So the way to get home, claims the book of Hebrews, is faith. Access is only by faith because faith alone corresponds to the contours of our true Home. If we seek from God "the city which is to come," faith is simply the most fitting way to seek it; for faith is "the assurance of things hoped for, the conviction of things not seen" linked with the belief that God exists and that He rewards those who seek Him (Hebrews 11:1,6). The Way Home is the way of faith---- faith animated by hope and crowned by love (I Corinthians 13:13).

While the way of faith is certainly not the only form the search for home takes in this world, it is the form toward which all the others point. No human family, no religious cult, no organization, no race and no civilization is capable of granting the permanent security many of them promise. Such security is possible, because we were made for it; but it is possible only in God and only through faith. This is why Christ designates Himself as what every human soul has been waiting for: "I am the way, the truth and the life" (John 14:6).

Faith in Him carries with it the power to resist perhaps the most potent mirage of earthly security we ever face: carnal religion. Carnal religion is fleshly spirituality, self-centeredness in religious garb. Any religious relic or shrine can induce it. The Christian cathedral has yet to be built that does not tempt the worshipper to retreat from the cross of Christ into the comfortable nest of worldly religion. At the moment, Christianity is the most powerful and influential religion on earth. And the more powerful the religion, the greater the temptation to focus on itself and on the haven it provides.

At least three types of carnal religion are alive and well in America today, and they all have ancient roots. Christianity first encountered politicized religion in the Roman Empire, and struggled mightily for centuries to desacralize the political sphere.[15] Its most common recent form in the West is when religious bodies officially endorse nationalism or any type of politically-sponsored violence. Instrumental religion, or a religion designed primarily to fulfill human needs other than the need for God (such as bodily health or success), is very popular in this pragmatic, "show me what works" country of ours. The skeptical philosopher, David Hume, took this to be the essence of all religion. A third type, the religion of the family, has been a focus of this book. The center of loyalty here tends to be the family itself and not the family's Creator.

Note that both the political and the familial types of carnal religion are usually forms of the search for home. All three types give a measure of real security to the believer. All are capable of masking their worldliness with religious language. And each type, if left unchecked, can have unhealthy consequences.

But what can check them? Secular perspectives----the skepticism of a Hume or a Bertrand Russell, the searchlight of science----have the knowledge but not the force. These carnal religions speak to the home-needs of the soul, needs running so deep that no secular alternative has the power to successfully challenge them. Only religion can. What we need today is exactly what the New Testament provides: drawing on Amos, Isaiah, and the entire tradition of Hebrew prophets, the New Testament writers present us with a new kind of religion, to wit, one that is suspicious of religion's own power. We need a religious Way and Light so true that it can spot the worldly shortcuts religion itself sponsors.

In Christ, early Christians saw that the world had been given the most exquisite of gifts----an altar on which the ancient need to make blood sacrifices had been brought to a close. What religion had been trying to do for millenia at last had been done, once and for all, in the suffering of one man on a lonely, secular hill "outside the gate" (Hebrews 13:12). Those who don't realize this will continue to go "into the sanctuary" (Hebrews 13:11) and make sacrifices for guilt and sin, as if this religious cycle had not been broken. But with eyes on Christ rather than the sanctuary, the way of faith leads Christians to "go forth to Him outside the camp" and make a new kind of sacrifice: bearing abuse for Him, continually praising God, and never neglecting to do good and to share what they have (Hebrews 13:13-16). Against all humanly-constructed havens of this world, the way of Christ is the Way Home.

NOTES

[1]Alexander Schmemann, For the Life of the World: Sacrements and Orthodoxy, 2nd Revised and Expanded Edition (New York: St. Vladimir's Seminary Press, 1973), p. 90.

[2]A sense of the ecclesial quality of family life is so strong in the Roman Catholic and Orthodox traditions that not only infant baptism but marriage and confirmation are given sacramental status. See, for example, Vigen Guroian, "An Ethic of Marriage and Family," Incarnate Love: Essays in Orthodox Ethics (Notre Dame, IN: University of Notre Dame Press, 1987), pp. 79-114. Though I finally disagree with Guroian's claim that marriage is a sacrament, this very conviction gives him access to splendid insights concerning the sacred dimension of the family. Protestant couples contemplating marriage should be required to read his essay.

[3]For a lucid restatement of this Protestant position, see Helmut Thielicke, Theological Ethics, Vol. 3: Sex, translated by J. W. Doberstein (Grand Rapids, MI: Eerdmans, 1979), pp. 101-144. I find Thielicke to be particularly instructive regarding the decisive issue of the relation between the orders of creation and redemption in marriage.

[4]Martin Luther, Selected Writings of Martin Luther, ed. by T. G. Tappert (Philadelphia: Fortress Press, 1967), p. 444.

[5]Ibid., p. 445.

[6]On the subtle and the massive consequences of this, see Paul Tillich's The Protestant Era, trans. by J. L. Adams (Chicago: University of Chicago Press, 1948).

[7]Here I am following Dietrich Bonhoeffer's assessment of Luther's teachings in Ethics, trans. by N. H. Smith (New York: Macmillan, 1955), pp. 94ff.

[8]This narrow definition is not characteristic of all or even most of the literature on secularization. The literature is vast. For some orientation in the area, see Phillip Hammond, ed., The Sacred in a Secular Age: Toward Revision in the Scientific Study of Religion (Berkeley, CA: University of California Press, 1985), and the bibliography in David Lyon's The Steeple's Shadow (London: SPCK, 1985). The most articulate exponent of classical secularization theory, with its assumption that secularization means religious decline, is Bryan Wilson. See his Religion in Sociological Perspective

(Oxford: Oxford University Press, 1982). For a series of attacks on the idea that this classical assumption is at all descriptive of recent U. S. history, see Richard Neuhaus, ed., Unsecular America (Grand Rapids: Eerdmans, 1986). Peter Berger's analysis of secularization in The Sacred Canopy (New York: Doubleday, 1967) remains influential. On the mistake of identifying secularization with increasing worldliness, see Hannah Arendt, The Human Condition, pp. 175-197. One of Paul Tillich's finest insights was that secularization in the West has meant not so much a reduction in religion's power as its diffusion. See his discussion of "quasi-religions" in Christianity and the Encounter of the World Religions (New York: Columbia University Press, 1963).

⁹The impact of secularization on the economic sphere is the subject of Max Weber's controversial masterpiece, The Protestant Ethic and the Spirit of Capitalism, trans. by T. Parsons (New York: Scribner, 1958). Though Weber is properly cautious about claiming either that a certain type of Protestant ethic caused the rise of capitalisim or vice versa, we may wish--as a general rule--to be even more cautious. As Mary Douglas has argued, allegedly scientific studies of the relation between religious beliefs and social influences are almost inevitably marked by cultural and theological bias. "The Effects of Modernization on Religious Change," Daedalus (Winter, 1982), pp. 1-20.

¹⁰I am drawing here from David Martin's A General Theory of Secularization (Oxford: Oxford University Press, 1978). A considerable strength of this book is Martin's refusal to use the category, "religion," in a vague, non-substantive way. Many secularization theories can be faulted at this very point. See Larry Shiner, "The Concept of Secularization in Empirical Research," Journal of the Scientific Study of Religion, Vol. VI, No. 2 (Fall, 1967), pp. 207-220.

¹¹James Burtchaell, For Better, For Worse, pp. 38f, 91ff.

¹²The point is made nicely by Rodney Clapp in "Is the Traditional Family Biblical?" Christianity Today (Sept. 16, 1988), pp. 24-28.

¹³The classical Christian statement on the relation between the one "Eternal City" and the many temporal ones is found in the work of Augustine. Composed between 414-426 A.D., his vast study shows, on the one hand, why political communities (in particular, the Roman state) are as strong as they are, and also why they can never endure without end. See The City of God in Volume Two of Basic Writings of Saint Augustine, edited by Whitney J. Oates (New York: Random House, 1948), esp. Book XIX.

[14]A quite remarkable exposition of the meaning of the "family of God," centered in a present and pervasive disposition of joy, can be found in Chapter 8 of Stan Hauerwas's book, The Peaceable Kingdom: A Primary in Christian Ethics (Southbend: University of Notre Dame Press, 1983) pp. 135-151. He writes: "Joy, we think, is spontaneous but has little staying power. It cannot sustain us over the long haul. But the joy we receive as Christians is not that of a passing occasion. Rather it is a joy that derives from finding our true home among a people who carry the words and skills of God's kingdom of peace" (p. 147).

[15]On the distinctiveness of early Christian thinking about politics as well as family, the best book I know is Charles Cochrane, Christianity and Classical Culture (New York: Oxford University Press, 1940).

EPILOGUE

As noted in the Preface, this book appears in the aftermath of the publication of a major denominational report on human sexuality. In its national meeting in June of 1991, the Presbyterian Church decided not to adopt the provocative and academically quite respectable report, though Presbyterians also decided to retain it for possible future use alongside other studies.[1] Since this two hundred page document has received such wide publicity, it might be useful briefly to compare it with the approach of the book before you.

By any standard, the Presbyterian Special Report on Human Sexuality calls for a revolutionary re-interpretation of classical Christian teaching on sex, marriage and family. To some extent, there is nothing new here. A good number of modern schools of theology require revisions of a similar sort. Feminist theology does. Black theology does. Liberation theology does.

This book does not. To help Christian parents today, I don't believe that the received Christian tradition needs to be changed all that much. The method in Out of Step has been to mine this tradition, apply it to modern families in context, and do both of these things with a certain attitude of reserve----an attitude any reader has a right to expect from an author attempting to unravel both the mysteries of family life and the mystery of God's activity in the world. Where I gain a good deal from the Presbyterian Report is through its extraordinary sensitivity to the social context of family life, and particularly to the destructive side of this context----patriarchal authoritarianism, poverty, racial discrimination, governmental indifference, and the like.

Put differently, there is an imbalance I detect in the Report that strikes me as similar to one found in most contemporary schools of Christian theology rooted in the social gospel tradition. They mistake a part for the whole. Were Paul Tillich alive, he might say that their Protestant principle tends to overwhelm their

Catholic substance. In terms of the Bible, they are too much the prophet and too little the priest. So when a Beverly W. Harrison or a James B. Nelson turns to the family, its sacredness is (apart from its idolatrous potential) of little interest to them.[2]

In the second place, Out of Step differs sharply from the Majority Presbyterian Report in its approach to diversity. Though the Report is helpful in recognizing the fact of theological diversity in the church today, it is not always clear what the authors believe this fact signifies. What they appear to mean by diversity and pluralism is this: the theological center of Christ's church no longer has any weight. If such a center exists, it exists only nominally in the sense that the majority of Christian believers happen to adhere to these particular standards in this time and in this place. They all could be wrong----about the Bible, about God, about Christ, about the church. Furthermore, according to the Report, orthodox theological ethics is almost assuredly wrong and out of touch whenever it is challenged from the left.

I embrace diversity too, but not in this manner. I find myself straddling a religious fence peculiar to the United States of America in the last half of the twentieth century. One foot is on the "conservative evangelical" side and the other in the "liberal" Christian camp. My own family of origin was located firmly in the former tradition, my intellectual training in the latter.

So the book is aimed at both these tribes. But I am no longer sure that they can be effectively addressed in a single voice. The fence is getting less and less comfortable each day, and there are fewer and fewer fellow travelers straddling it with me. As Robert Wuthnow's fine book on the subject indicates, the cultural gap between these two camps is now a profound one, and shows few signs of narrowing.[3]

Thirdly, there is the question of the proper audience for Out of Step and for the Presbyterian Report. The Report is best received in an academic context. It should be studied in an intellectual setting diverse enough to ensure that other points of view on the same subject will be considered as well. It brings together expert testimony on an extraordinarily wide variety of sexual issues and problems. The data will have great value for courses and research on sexual ethics.

Out of Step, also, will contribute to academic discussion. But throughout this book, the reader will sense a persistent suspicion of the tendency to resolve uncertainty about our families by turning to experts. My central claim about the family----that it is "sacred"----is meant to check this tendency. No matter how frequently we analyze it, family life remains irreducibly mysterious for ourselves as parents and for our children as well. Uncertainty is not only a possible response to mystery but the correct response; it is one of the family's most precious possessions. When we go to psychologists, to sociologists, to other academics and even to ministers for help with our families, we should do it with a pinch of humor and some skepticism, and with a reminder to ourselves that there are few absolutely clear answers in this life.

In sum, O gentle reader, I would leave you with three suggestions. The first is not to forget the genius of the biblical perspective on the family. In the Bible, most so-called "family problems" turn out to be of a deeper, more basic type: human problems. I have found this to be true in my own life. When the Bible does focus on the family (as in the story of Jacob and Esau, or of Joseph, or of David), we encounter the strangely comforting truth that there are no perfect families. We don't meet idealized portrayals of the family in Scripture, but instead the family as it actually is----a series of broken relationships in need of redemption.

A second suggestion is to turn to strong families in your acquaintance. They exist in every neighborhood, no matter how oppressive the material or social conditions. A healthy family is a work of art. Watch it, sit with it, listen to it, learn from it. You may learn more in a day from an actual strong family than from a month's worth of family dynamics classes.

And there is one more author I would commend to you. When Pulitzer Prize winner Robert Coles talks about the family, he speaks with his heart as well as his head. Coles spent much of his life observing and working with children and their families----young black children who integrated southern schools; the children of migrants, Native Americans and sharecroppers oppressed by racism and poverty; and most recently the children of war-torn Northern Ireland and racially segregated South Africa. His multi-volume work, The Children of Crisis, is not written in the lingo of his profession of psychology, but in the plain language of common sense.[4]

In these books, we become re-acquainted with the extraordinary moral, intellectual, emotional and spiritual resources of ordinary people. We are reminded that no amount of scientific analysis was ever meant to take the place of the kaffee-klatsch, of one's neighbors, of one's friends. We remember that to be an imperfect parent is not necessarily to fail as a parent. In unaffected prose, Coles describes the deeply human qualities of labor, loyalty, humility, discipline, piety and love that have always made the family tick, qualities to which the wisest family experts can only point----and ultimately defer.

NOTES

¹See David Heim's insightful report on the meeting, "Sexual Congress: The Presbyterian Debate," Christian Century (June 26-July 3, 1991), pp. 643-644.

²See, for example, Beverly Harrison, Making the Connections: Essays in Feminist Social Ethics, Carol Robb ed. (Boston, MA: Beacon Press, 1985), pp. 42ff, 115ff; and James Nelson, Between Two Gardens, pp. 128ff.

³Robert Wuthnow, The Struggle for America's Soul: Evangelicals, Liberals and Secularlism (Grand Rapids, MI: Eerdmans, 1989).

⁴Robert Coles, The Children of Crisis, Vol I: A Study of Fear and Courage (Boston, MA: Little, Brown, 1967); Vol. II: Migrants, Sharecroppers, Mountaineers (Boston, MA: Little, Brown, 1971); Vol. III: The South Goes North (Boston, MA: Little, Brown, 1971); Vol. IV: Eskimos, Chicanos, Indians (Boston, MA: Little, Brown, 1980); Vol. V: Privileged Ones: The Well-off and the Rich in America (Boston, MA: Little, Brown, 1978). Also his The Spiritual Life of Children (Boston, MA: Houghton Mifflin, 1990) is worth a look.

ABOUT THE AUTHOR

Wayne G. Boulton is Professor of Religion and Department Chair at Hope College in Holland, Michigan. Born in South Carolina and raised just north of New York City, he was ordained to the Presbyterian ministry in 1970. He received his B.A. from Lafayette College, his M.Div. from McCormick Theological Seminary, and his Ph.D. from Duke University. He has published articles in journals such as Christian Century and Theology Today. This is his second book.